FOOD

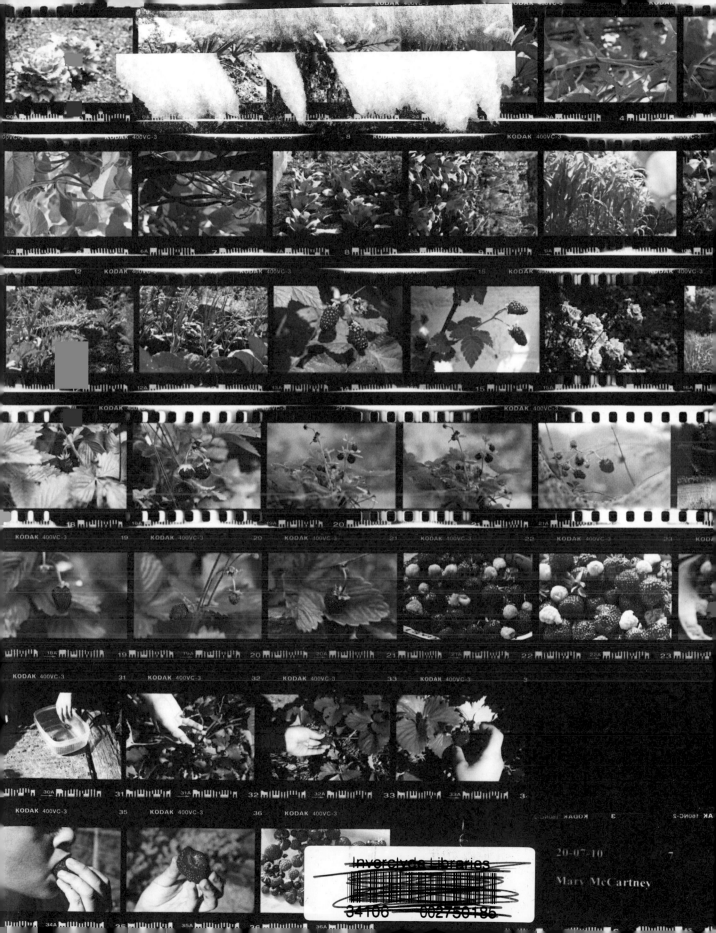

20-07-10   7

Mary McCartney

MARY McCARTNEY FOOD

Chatto & Windus
LONDON

Published by Chatto & Windus 2012

2 4 6 8 10 9 7 5 3 1

Text and photographs copyright © Mary McCartney 2012

Photo of Mary on back jacket © Simon Aboud
Photo of Mary on p.IV © Alex Foreman
Photo of Mary on pp.XII and 69 © Arthur Donald
Photographs on pp.VII and XI © Paul McCartney
Photographs on pp.VIII, IX, X and XVI by Linda McCartney, © Paul McCartney

First published in Great Britain in 2012 by
Chatto & Windus
Random House, 20 Vauxhall Bridge Road,
London SW1V 2SA
www.vintage-books.co.uk

Addresses for companies within The Random House Group Limited can be found at:
www.randomhouse.co.uk/offices.htm

The Random House Group Limited Reg. No. 954009

A CIP catalogue record for this book is available from the British Library

ISBN 9780701186258
Art direction and design: Jesse Holborn / Design Holborn

The Random House Group Limited supports The Forest Stewardship Council®(FSC®), the leading international forest certification organisation. Our books carrying the FSC label are printed on FSC® certified paper. FSC is the only forest certification scheme endorsed by the leading environmental organisations, including Greenpeace. Our paper procurement policy can be found at www.randomhouse.co.uk/environment

Printed and bound in China by C&C Offset Printing Co., Ltd.

*Me and Mum, Scotland, 1971 — and the beginning
of my journey with a passion for food.*

INTRODUCTION

I have a confession to make. By profession I'm a photographer not a cook, but cooking is something I love to do. So I have been lucky enough to combine my two passions and have written and photographed almost everything in this book. By indulging both my great loves, I have found myself more immersed in this project than perhaps I thought possible when the idea for the book was taking shape, and I have loved the process. Getting the recipe right, cooking it and then immediately photographing the result at home has made this a truly organic, cottage industry. A friend even jokingly suggested I buy a printing press for the next one!

My husband and our friends were the ones who first made me seriously consider writing my own cookbook – they're always asking me to write down my recipes and say that I seem to 'magic it up' out of nowhere while chatting to them. But, really, I think my feel for vegetarian cooking is so ingrained that it has become second nature. Growing up in a vegetarian family and having Mum at the helm in the kitchen, encouraging us all to muck in, was the best education I could have asked for. My whole family are real foodies because everything we ate as we grew up was simply delicious and all of it was hassle-free, quick and uncomplicated. As the years have gone by I have continued to cook as my mum did, constantly experimenting with different combinations of ingredients, flavours and textures. I have added my own touches and refined the recipes over time. Up until now these have stayed in my head; I'm not disciplined at writing anything down, so often a meal will be made once – enjoyed – and then forgotten.

I suppose this is part of my motivation for embarking on this project. It has made me take the time to write down measurements and methods and really think about my earliest childhood food memories and inspirations.

I like uncomplicated cooking, so usually it needs to be kept quite simple and not too time-consuming. I enjoy cooking with friends and family around me; it's certainly a social activity for me. When friends come over I don't go overboard trying to concoct culinary masterpieces, but stick to my usual cooking style which is relaxed, straightforward and stress-free – the empty plates at the end of a meal tell me they are happy!

I think our early experiences and memories of food determine so much of our approach to it as we get older. I was lucky enough to enjoy a very varied vegetarian diet and so, for me, it wasn't limiting because there was always choice. My siblings and I were involved in the experience of cooking from a very early age. The kitchen was the centre of the universe and Mum got us involved, helping to cook and tasting…always tasting. Now with my own children, I try to get them involved. We discuss meals and recipe ideas and flavour combinations, and I have found that it gives them a point of view and demystifies the process. The more involved they are, the more interested they become in food and cooking.

When we were young, Mum let us choose our favourite meal on our birthdays. I often chose her cream of tomato soup and fluffy quiche with a large mixed salad. And now I let my kids do the same. I want that tradition to continue and I hope that involving them shows them how varied and tasty a vegetarian diet can be. I have included their favourite recipes – fresh pesto, quiche, tomato sauce, chocolate chip cookies, pavlova and many more – in this book, and these are recipes that they have started to make for me! I hope this book encourages you and your children to have a go, too.

Many of the recipes in this book can be adapted and tweaked to your own taste, and if certain ingredients are not available (due to seasonality or logistics) usually others can be substituted instead; you don't have to be a slave to the recipe.

Cooking has always been about a mixture of things for me: eclectic influences, places, tastes and ingredients that together form my own view of food and how it all goes together. But, above all, two people in my life have provided the foundation for my cooking style.

My main cooking influence was my mother, Linda. She described herself as a peasant cook and had the ability to transform whatever she found in the pantry into delicious meals. Her style was pretty laid-back and low maintenance. Being an American, the basis of her cooking was quite traditional and therefore so is mine; I guess I learnt by osmosis. I love making hearty soups, stews, fluffy rising quiches, large chef's salads and baked macaroni cheese. Mum also influenced my love of snacks; deep-filled New York deli-style sandwiches, grab bags to snack on during long journeys, filled with nuts, raisins and little chocolate pieces. One of my lasting memories of Mum is the two of us snacking on a well-tried and tested favourite of hers – rye toast with crunchy peanut butter and jam…alongside a hot cup of our favourite English breakfast tea.

When I was growing up I spent lots of happy times cooking and chatting with my mother. During those times I soaked up her knowledge, and gained an understanding of how certain extra-simple ingredients or cooking techniques could transform an ordinary dish into something special.

Her love of food was infectious but never precious. She never seemed to write anything down, a trick I inherited but which made the creation of this book particularly testing! My dad has also played his part in developing my cooking style as he would encourage us to come up with ideas to fill the 'hole' in a vegetarian's plate – like still having Sunday roasts and not feeling cheated while others tuck into their roast beef.

From a more technical point of view, the other culinary influence in my life was my French/American step-grandmother, Monique. She had been brought up as a stickler for rules and technique. As a child I found her quite austere, but when I hit my early twenties we found cooking as a common interest, and I am glad I took the time to cook with her and learn from some of her teachings. She was very precise, and collected recipes and measured ingredients methodically. This was completely new to me. She taught me how to make and roll pastry, and she inspired my enduring love of baking. She even got me hooked on using an oven thermometer to ensure the oven was accurate and at the right heat.

These influences and memories are so warm and colourful and they have informed the type of cook I have become. I love feeding friends and family, and getting everyone round the table together – the banter around informal meals and the satisfaction of wiped-clean plates. There was nothing boring about food when I grew up and now I just want to share some of this passion in the hope that you'll find vegetarian food as enticing, varied and delicious as I have done all these years.

It has been a challenge balancing the desire to create something new and exciting with the rigour of writing down a new recipe. With that in mind, my wonderfully encouraging Aunt Louise bought me a beautiful wooden recipe box. Now when I make something new that is a success, and my husband despairs, wondering if I'll ever remember to make it again, I can write it down on a card and put it straight into the recipe box (well, most of the time!). This always makes me smile and raise a glass to my mum.

Mary

Note from my mum on the fridge.

COOKING NOTES

AL DENTE PASTA AND VEGETABLES

I like pasta and most vegetables to be cooked 'al dente' – an Italian expression meaning 'to the bite' or 'to the tooth' – so that they are still slightly firm and not too soggy. It's a good idea to taste the pasta or vegetable when you think it is almost ready – and take a bite. Basically, you want to feel a little resistance in the centre.

BLIND BAKING

The recipes in this book that use pastry involve blind baking (pre-baking) the pastry case before you put the filling in, because this is the best way to help prevent the base of the pie crust from becoming too soggy and doughy.

FREEZING

I often make too much and then freeze what we don't eat, so I've always got the good stuff ready in the freezer. Foodstuffs that freeze well are soups, vegetable stocks, gravy, shepherd's pie, lasagne, sauces, etc. I also like to have an emergency supply of bagels and bread, and milk. When freezing liquids do not overfill containers, as liquid expands when frozen. Baked goods, such as biscuits, muffins and cakes, freeze well too. There are foods that don't freeze well, such as vegetables with a high water content, for example cucumber, cabbage, oranges, lettuce, celery and onion. Egg-based sauces won't work that well either, but dairy products such as milk, butter and cream can be frozen. Over time, your freezer can become an Aladdin's cave of hidden treasures waiting for the right moment.

INGREDIENTS

• **VEGETARIAN CHEESES**: There is a wide variety of cheeses that are suitable for vegetarians, and they are now much more widely available in local shops and supermarkets. These cheeses are made without using animal rennet (animal rennet is not vegetarian as it is an enzyme that comes from the stomachs of animals). Parmesan can sometimes be more difficult to find. Bookhams does a great Parmesan-style cheese (http://bookhams.com) that can be bought in wedges (rather than the pre-grated stuff, which I find lacks taste), and it keeps well frozen for up to five months. If you cannot find Parmesan, then a good sharp hard cheese will substitute perfectly well.

INGREDIENTS

- **VEGETARIAN MINCE, SAUSAGES AND BURGERS**: These are available from specialist health food shops and some supermarkets. I use vegetarian sausages and soya mince (vege-mince®) from the Linda McCartney Foods range (see http://www.lindamccartneyfoods.co.uk for stockists). All products in the range are suitable for vegetarians and contain no GMOs (genetically modified organisms) or trans fats. The sausages and burgers can be grilled, barbecued or added to casseroles and stews, while the mince is perfect for using in dishes such as shepherd's pie, spaghetti bolognese, lasagne and chilli con carne.

- **EGGS**: In all the recipes in this book I recommend using large, free-range eggs (preferably organic too), but if you use medium-sized ones I don't think it will cause any huge problems. I use free-range eggs rather than eggs produced by hens kept in cages in factory farms. The move to free-range eggs by many consumers has seen a huge positive change in suppliers replacing factory eggs with free-range. Let's keep up the pressure.

- **SUGAR**: I like to use natural granulated or caster sugar. Unrefined cane sugar is a good alternative to bleached white refined sugar. Billingtons (http://www.billingtons.co.uk) is a good brand and quite widely available.

- **VANILLA**: These recipes use vanilla extract NOT vanilla essence. Vanilla extract is made by soaking vanilla beans in alcohol and water so that the flavour is infused into the liquid. It can be expensive, but keeps in the fridge for a long time while retaining its flavour.

- **VEGETABLE STOCK**: I have included a fresh vegetable stock recipe if you want to make your own. It can be kept in the fridge for up to 5 days, and it freezes well too. I also often use Marigold reduced-salt Swiss vegetable bouillon powder instead of fresh stock.

- **COOKING CHOCOLATE AND COCOA POWDER**: I like to use Green and Black's plain dark chocolate 70%, although there are several great-quality chocolate brands available. I think, for cooking, as long as you stick to 70% cocoa content, then it should be fine.

• **SPELT FLOUR**: I have started to use spelt organic stoneground white flour in place of plain flour (although either will do). Spelt flour is an ancient wheat variety which is meant to be easily digestible. The white spelt flour has been sieved from the coarse outer layers of the bran and has a similar texture to plain flour. You can turn both spelt and plain flour into self-raising by adding 2 teaspoons of baking powder per every 250g flour.

• **GELATINE SUBSTITUTE**: Agar flakes are a great substitute to gelatine. Agar is a gelling agent derived from seaweed. Sanchi (http://www.sanchi.co.uk) is a good brand. You can also buy really tasty classic jelly mixes in various flavours that use natural colours and no gelatine, such as vegetarian jelly crystals made by Just Wholefoods (http://www.justwholefoods.co.uk). Gelatine is not vegetarian as it is made from the boiled bones, skins and tendons of animals.

CONVERSION TABLES

OVEN TEMPERATURES

°F	°C	Gas Mark
275	140	1
300	150	2
325	160/170	3
350	180	4
375	190	5
400	200	6
425	220	7

WEIGHT

Ounces (oz)	Grams (g)
½	15
1	25
1½	45
2	55
2½	70
3	85
4	115
5	140
6	170
7	200
8	225
12	340
1lb	455
1lb 8 oz	680
2lb	910

LIQUIDS

Fl.oz (pints)	Millilitres (litres)
2	60
3	90
4	120
5 (¼ pint)	140
6	180
7	205
8	230
10 (½ pint)	290
12	340
14	400
15	430
20 (1 pint)	570
2 pints	1.1l
1 tablespoon	(½ fl.oz/15ml)
2 tablespoons	(1 fl.oz/30ml)
3 tablespoons	(1½ fl.oz/45ml)
4 tablespoons	(2 fl.oz/60ml)
6 tablespoons	(3 fl.oz/85ml)
8 tablespoons	(4 fl.oz/115ml)

BREAKFAST AND BRUNCH

FRUIT AND NUT GRANOLA

I always used to buy granola, until a friend showed me how easy and satisfying it is to make. What I love about it is that once you've made the syrup and measured out the oats you can modify the other ingredients to your own taste, by using your own choice of nuts and seeds and dried fruit (sticking roughly to the specified 50g for each ingredient). Or you can stick with this recipe, which I think is well balanced and has a lovely roasted flavour. I love to serve this with a big spoonful of plain yogurt and some blueberries on top.

MAKES APPROX. 750G

INGREDIENTS

· 250g porridge oats, preferably jumbo oats
· 45g brazil nuts (approx. 10 nuts), roughly chopped
· 50g sunflower seeds, roughly chopped
· 50g pumpkin seeds, roughly chopped
· 50g dried apricots, chopped
· 50g raisins
· 50g dried cranberries

For the syrup:
· 3 tablespoons sunflower or cooking oil
· 5½ tablespoons maple syrup
· 5½ tablespoons runny honey

METHOD

· Preheat your oven to 150°C/gas mark 2. Line 2 baking trays with baking parchment or greaseproof paper.
· In a large mixing bowl combine the oats, brazil nuts, sunflower and pumpkin seeds. Set this aside while you make the syrup.
· To make the syrup pour the oil, maple syrup and honey into a small saucepan and heat gently until warm but not bubbling, stirring well until all the ingredients are mixed together. Take care not to let it bubble and overcook.
· Drizzle the syrup over the oats, nuts and seeds and mix together so that all the ingredients are lightly coated.
· Spread the mixture out evenly over the 2 baking trays, so that it is about 1.5cm deep. Bake for 30–40 minutes, taking it out of the oven 2 times during baking to mix the granola around and then return it to continue baking. When it's ready it should be golden brown.
· Take the granola out of the oven and now mix in the apricots, raisins and cranberries.
· Set it aside to cool, then store in an airtight container and keep in a cool dry place until needed (stored like this, it will keep for 2–3 weeks).

FRUITY OMEGA SMOOTHIES

These smoothies are an easy and refreshing way of getting those essential omega oils into your diet. I like to use frozen strawberries – they last well and help to keep the smoothie nice and cold. You can buy the omega oil in most supermarkets or local health food shops.

STAWBERRY AND BANANA

MAKES 4

INGREDIENTS

· 2 bananas
· 8 frozen strawberries
· 400ml fresh apple juice
· 2 tablespoons Omega 3 6 9 oil

METHOD

· Peel the bananas, then break them in half or chop roughly into quarters before putting them in your blender. Add the frozen strawberries and then pour in the apple juice and omega oil. Blend until smooth, which should take about I minute.
· Pour the smoothie into whatever glasses or cups you're using, and serve immediately while it's still cold.

TROPICAL PINEAPPLE AND COCONUT

MAKES 4

INGREDIENTS

· ¼ pineapple, peeled, cored and cut into chunks (you could use tinned if you don't have fresh, approx. 250g)
· 8 tablespoons coconut milk
· 400ml fresh orange juice
· 2 tablespoons Omega 3 6 9 oil

METHOD

· Place all the ingredients in a blender and blitz well, for about I minute, until smooth.
· Pour the smoothie into whatever glasses or cups you're using, and serve immediately.

GRANOLA BAR TO GO

This is my favourite guilt-free snack for breakfasts on the go, packed lunches or just to have in your bag for stolen snacky moments. And as it cooks it fills your home with the wonderful smell of fresh home baking.

MAKES 12–14 PIECES

INGREDIENTS

- 200ml agave syrup
- 50g butter
- 4 tablespoons vegetable oil
- ¼ teaspoon ground cinnamon
- I tablespoon vanilla extract
- 200g porridge oats
- 80g cornflakes
- 100g almonds, coarsely chopped
- 100g dried apricots, coarsely chopped
- 100g raisins or sultanas
- 2 tablespoons sunflower seeds
- 2 tablespoons pumpkin seeds

METHOD

- Line a baking tray (approx. 30 x 20cm) with greaseproof paper or baking parchment. Preheat your oven to 180°C/gas mark 4.
- In a large saucepan, gently simmer the agave syrup for about 4 minutes, to allow it to turn a bit syrupy (be careful, this is very hot). Take it off the heat and then add the butter and vegetable oil, stirring well until the butter has melted. Add the cinnamon and vanilla extract and then mix in the oats, cornflakes, almonds, apricots, raisins, sunflower and pumpkin seeds. Stir well to ensure that all the ingredients are coated in the syrup.
- Spoon the granola mix into the baking tray and push it down so that it's evenly packed into the tray.
- Bake it in the oven for 15–20 minutes, until the top is turning golden.
- Take the tray out of the oven and leave the granola to cool before lifting it out of the baking tray, cutting it into pieces and then peeling off the baking paper.

BANANA MUFFINS

MAKES 10–12 MUFFINS

INGREDIENTS

· 275g plain or spelt flour
· 2 teaspoons baking powder
· 80g sugar, preferably unrefined caster or granulated
· 1 large, free-range egg
· 3 large or 4 medium ripe bananas, mashed well
· 1 teaspoon vanilla extract
· 100g soured cream or crème fraîche
· 100g melted butter

· 10–12 muffin cases

METHOD

· Preheat your oven to 180°C/gas mark 4. Place the muffin cases into a 12-hole non-stick muffin tin.
· Put all the ingredients into a large mixing bowl and beat together until well combined. You can use a food processor for this if preferred.
· Divide the mixture equally between the muffin cases.
· Bake for 20 minutes, until the tops have turned golden and are just firm to the touch. I think these are best served warm — but they can be kept for about 3 days in an airtight container.

QUICK BREAKFAST BOWL

SERVES 1

INGREDIENTS

· 4 tablespoons muesli or granola
· 1 tablespoon flax seeds or linseeds (optional)
· 4 tablespoons plain live yogurt
· 1 medium banana, thinly sliced
· 2 tablespoons blueberries, or 4 sliced strawberries (or another seasonal fruit of your choice), chopped into bite-sized pieces (optional)
· 5 walnuts, broken into pieces
· 1 tablespoon runny honey or maple syrup

METHOD

· Spoon the muesli or granola into a large breakfast bowl, sprinkle the flax seeds or linseeds (if using) over the cereal then spoon the plain yogurt on top. Arrange the banana, blueberries (or other fruit) and nuts over the top and, finally, drizzle with the runny honey or maple syrup. And it's ready!

FRENCH TOAST

One of my favourite weekend breakfast dishes, this is something I grew up eating, but didn't actually learn how to make until I was in my early 20s. I must have assumed it was more complicated to make than it really is. It's perfect as a satisfying special breakfast or brunch for family and friends when you have only a few eggs, milk and some bread that's past its best in your larder — suddenly these ingredients are transformed into an indulgent golden delight when the generous drizzle of pure maple syrup is poured over the top. My dad grew up calling it 'eggy bread', and his family never ate it sweet with maple syrup; instead they had tomato ketchup on the side. You can experiment by using different types of bread, although I usually stick to thickly sliced wholegrain, organic white or multigrain bread that's not too fresh or soft. And you can vary the flavour, if you like, by adding a pinch of ground cinnamon or a teaspoon of vanilla extract or orange zest to the eggy mix.

SERVES 4

INGREDIENTS

- 3 large, free-range eggs
- 600ml semi-skimmed milk
- butter, for frying
- 8 slices bread, preferably thick-sliced and a couple of days old
- pure maple syrup, to serve

METHOD

- In a wide shallow bowl (wide enough to fit a slice of bread), beat together the eggs and milk until well blended.
- Take a large non-stick frying pan and heat it to medium high. When it is hot, add a small amount of butter and tilt it around the pan to melt and lightly cover the pan base.
- Dip the bread, 1 slice at a time, into the mixture and allow it to soak up some of the eggy milk on both sides (but don't let it get too soggy).
- Gently place as many slices of the soaked bread into the hot pan as will comfortably fit and fry for a couple of minutes on each side, using a slotted (metal, rubber or plastic) turner to flip the bread. Fry until a deep golden brown on both sides.
- Serve immediately with maple syrup drizzled over the top, or you can make this in batches, keeping some slices warm in a low-heated oven while you soak and fry the remaining pieces.

RHUBARB COMPOTE

SERVES APPROX. 4

INGREDIENTS

- 400g rhubarb, trimmed
- 4 tablespoons unrefined sugar or agave syrup
- juice of 1 orange

METHOD

- Rinse the rhubarb stems and cut them into 2cm pieces. Put the rhubarb into a medium saucepan, add the sugar or syrup and pour in the freshly squeezed orange juice.
- Simmer gently on a medium heat for about 8–10 minutes, until the rhubarb is cooked through but still holds its shape. Transfer into a bowl. Once cooled, it can be kept in the fridge for up to 3 days.

HEARTY PORRIDGE

SERVES 2–3

INGREDIENTS

- 100g jumbo porridge oats
- 300ml milk or soya milk
- 300ml water
- 1 tablespoon linseeds
- 1 tablespoon finely chopped mixed sunflower and pumpkin seeds
- runny honey or maple syrup (approx. 1 tablespoon per bowl), for drizzling on top
- chopped seasonal fruit or berries, for sprinkling on top (optional)

METHOD

- Place the oats in a medium saucepan and mix in the milk and water. Bring to the boil and gently simmer for 5–10 minutes, stirring often to stop the porridge sticking to the pan.
- Once the porridge is cooked, take the pan off the heat and add the linseeds and the sunflower/pumpkin seeds mix. Stir well and pour into breakfast bowls.
- Drizzle maple syrup or runny honey over the porridge.
- Serve hot, topped with some chopped fruit or berries, if you like.

BREAKFAST PANCAKES

Many of my favourite memories of Mum involve food – cooking together and then chatting as we ate. One morning, we were both home alone so we decided to cook blueberry pancakes, poured a generous amount of maple syrup over them, then got back into bed to eat and watched the classic film La Dolce Vita.

This recipe is for classic American breakfast pancakes, but you can add a handful or two of blueberries to the batter if you like. If you don't have plain flour or baking powder you can use self-raising flour as a substitute.

MAKES ABOUT 16 PANCAKES

INGREDIENTS

- 120g plain or spelt flour
- 1½ teaspoons baking powder
- 2 large, free-range eggs
- 200ml semi-skimmed milk
- 2 teaspoons vegetable, sunflower or olive oil
- 2 teaspoons butter
- maple syrup, to serve

METHOD

- Sift the flour and baking powder into a medium/large mixing bowl or food processor. Make a well in the centre of the flour, crack the 2 eggs into it and beat well. Slowly pour in the milk, beating constantly (so you don't get lumps). Keep beating until all the milk is mixed in and your batter is a smooth, creamy consistency — it should be light with a few air bubbles. Stir in the 2 teaspoons of oil.
- When the pancake mix is ready, heat a large, non-stick frying pan and melt in the butter.
- Check the pan is hot enough to cook the pancakes by dropping a tiny amount of the batter into the pan — if it sizzles, the pan's ready.
- Now pour the batter into the pan, 1 tablespoon at a time, and make pancakes about 6cm in diameter — spooning in batches of 4 if the frying pan size allows.
- When you notice small bubbles appearing on the surface, use a rubber or metal spatula to slightly lift the edges of the pancakes to check that the underside has turned golden brown. Then flip them over and cook the other side until that, too, is golden brown and cooked through.
- Slide the pancakes onto plates and serve hot with maple syrup poured on top.

SAUCY GRILLED MUSHROOMS AND TOMATOES ON TOAST

I love these for a weekend breakfast or brunch. They are really tasty and satisfying, and because they are grilled you can feel quite self-righteous about the whole thing. Great with scrambled eggs.

SERVES 2

INGREDIENTS

- 10 button mushrooms
- 8 cherry tomatoes or 2 medium tomatoes
- 2 tablespoons light olive oil
- 2 tablespoons soy sauce
- 3 sprigs thyme, rinsed and leaves removed, or 1 teaspoon dried thyme or mixed herbs
- 2 cloves garlic, finely chopped, or 1 teaspoon garlic granules
- 2–4 slices bread
- butter, for the toast
- black pepper, to taste

METHOD

- Heat the grill to medium high.
- Clean off any gritty bits from the mushrooms, cut back the stems and arrange the mushrooms on a baking tray. Cut the tomatoes in half and arrange them on the tray with the mushrooms.
- Drizzle the olive oil and soy sauce evenly over the mushrooms and tomatoes. Sprinkle with the herbs and chopped garlic.
- Place the tray under the grill to cook for 8–10 minutes, until the mushrooms and tomatoes look cooked through and the juices are bubbling in the baking tray.
- In the meantime toast and butter your slices of bread.
- When they're ready, arrange the mushrooms and tomatoes on the toast, and add a grind or two of black pepper to taste.

DEEP-FILLED OMELETTE

My mum would often make this omelette to eat at brunch on the weekends but I sometimes make it for a quick supper too. I love the thick brightly coloured tomato filling — it makes it really special and satisfying. It's perfect served with freshly buttered multigrain toast.

SERVES 2

INGREDIENTS

- 2 tablespoons cooking vegetable oil
- 2 medium onions, thinly sliced
- I stick celery, trimmed and finely chopped (optional)
- 4 mushrooms, thinly sliced
- 400g tin chopped tomatoes
- I teaspoon dried herbs (such as sage, parsley or thyme) or I tablespoon fresh
- sea salt and black pepper, to taste
- 4 large, free-range eggs
- I tablespoon butter
- 50g mature Cheddar, grated (optional)

METHOD

- To make the filling heat the oil in a medium or large frying pan, then add the onion slices and sauté for 5 minutes. Add the celery and cook gently for a further 2 minutes, stirring frequently. Mix in the mushrooms and sauté for another 5–8 minutes, until the juice from the mushrooms has evaporated and the mushrooms start to turn golden brown.
- Mix in the tin of tomatoes and the herbs, and season with sea salt and black pepper to taste. Simmer gently for 20 minutes, checking and stirring often. The sauce should reduce down and thicken nicely. Set aside while you make the omelette.
- Crack the eggs into a mixing bowl and beat them well. In a large frying pan, melt the butter over a medium to high heat.
- Once the pan and butter are hot, but not burning, pour in the eggs and swirl them around the base of the pan to coat it evenly. Season with black pepper and sprinkle the cheese (if using) over the eggs. Allow the eggs to cook through and the edges and bottom of the omelette to turn golden brown. You can finish cooking it under the grill if necessary. Once it's cooked, take the pan off the heat and spoon the heated tomato mixture onto one half of the omelette. Fold it over and cut it in half. Slide onto 2 plates.
- Serve hot.

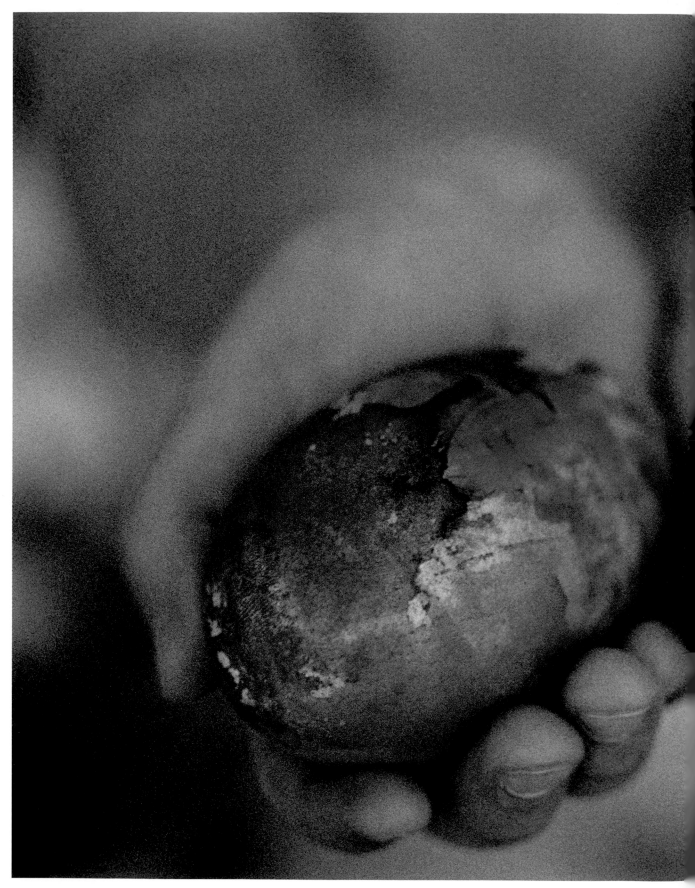

SNACKS AND SANDWICHES

HUMMOUS, AVOCADO AND CHILLI JAM SANDWICH

This sandwich combination is so moreish, it makes my mouth water just looking at the recipe.

SERVES I

INGREDIENTS

· **2 slices of sandwich bread, preferably a seeded or wholegrain loaf**
· **2 tablespoons hummous**
· **I tablespoon chilli jam**
· **½ hass avocado, peeled, stoned and thinly sliced**
· **squeeze of lemon juice**
· **small handful lettuce leaves**
· **sea salt and black pepper, to taste**

METHOD

· **Spread the 2 slices of bread with I tablespoon each of hummous. Spread the chilli jam on top of I slice, and then arrange a layer of avocado slices on top of that. Squeeze a little lemon juice over the avocado, then layer the lettuce leaves on top and season with a little sea salt and black pepper to taste. Sandwich the other slice of hummous bread on top, and eat immediately. Yum.**

PAN-FRIED
TORTILLA SANDWICH

The melty cheese, avocado and chilli kick make this one of my favourite lunchtime snacks. It's great served with a salad, such as the Sprouting Carrot Salad on p.85. It is simple to make, and so comforting to eat.

SERVES I

INGREDIENTS

· 2 corn or flour tortillas (approx. 20cm)
· 6 slices sharp cheese, such as goat's Cheddar, mature Cheddar, Red Leicester or similar (approx. 80g)
· ½ ripe hass avocado, peeled, stoned and cut into lcm slices
· I spring onion, trimmed and finely chopped
· ½ fresh red chilli, chopped, or ¼ teaspoon dried chilli flakes
· squeeze of fresh lime juice (approx. ½ teaspoon)
· pinch sea salt and freshly ground black pepper

METHOD

· Heat a medium non-stick frying pan over a medium heat and lay in I tortilla. Next, place the cheese slices evenly across the tortilla, then the avocado slices, followed by the spring onion and chilli and, finally, a squeeze of lime juice and sea salt and black pepper to taste. Then lay the second tortilla on top to form your sandwich.
· Once the underside of the tortilla sandwich has been fried for a minute or so, flip it over carefully. Allow the second side to cook through for a minute or until the cheese has gone melty. Eat hot.

PAN-FRIED CHEESE, TOMATO AND ONION SANDWICH

This recipe makes one sandwich — simple, quick, melty and indulgent. I love it served with coleslaw.

SERVES 1

INGREDIENTS

· 2 slices sandwich bread
· butter (approx. 15g), for the bread
· 6 slices cheese, such as mature Cheddar, goat's Cheddar, Red Leicester, Gouda
· 2 thin slices red onion
· 4 thin slices medium ripe tomato
· freshly ground black pepper, to taste

METHOD

· Butter both slices of bread and lay them, butter-side down, on a chopping board. Lay the cheese on to one of the slices of bread (unbuttered side), then top with the onion, tomato and black pepper. Finally, place the second piece of bread, butter-side up, on top.
· Put a medium frying pan over a medium to high heat. When the pan is hot place the sandwich, butter-side down, in the pan. Fry on one side until it's golden brown, about 2 minutes, occasionally pushing down the sandwich to help melt the cheese, then flip over the sandwich and fry on the second side for another couple of minutes until that's golden brown too and the cheese has melted.

Peanut butter, sliced banana and honey on toast.

Mature cheddar and coleslaw on seeded bread.

Toasted bagel with Marmite and hummus.

Falafel, hummus, chopped tomato and fresh mint, with a squeeze of lemon.

Sliced avocado, grated carrot, alfalfa sprouts and thousand island dressing.

Club sandwich: sliced boiled egg, fried halloumi, sliced red onion, tomato lettuce, mayo, mustard.

Soft goats cheese, fresh basil leaves, sliced marinated artichoke, sundried tomato, black pepper.

Veggi burger, cheese, crisp lettuce, sliced gherkin, tomato ketchup, mayo, mustard.

WARM AUBERGINE SANDWICH FILLING

This is a warm, comforting sandwich that I particularly enjoy on a rainy afternoon; it really has the ability to cheer me up when it is grey. The chilli flakes provide optional extra heat, if you are in the mood for a bit of spice. And a tasty alternative to the feta cheese is a mix of 2 tablespoons of tahini paste with 1 tablespoon of lemon juice – drizzle this over the warm aubergine filling once it is spooned onto the sandwich.

SERVES 2

INGREDIENTS

· 2 tablespoons light olive oil
· I medium onion, thinly sliced
· I medium aubergine, cut into bite-sized cubes
· ½ teaspoon soy sauce
· 6 sundried tomatoes, chopped
· I teaspoon finely chopped fresh parsley or oregano, or ½ teaspoon dried oregano
· small pinch dried chilli flakes (optional)
· French bread or crusty rolls
· butter, for the bread
· 100g feta cheese, crumbled
· squeeze of fresh lemon juice (½ lemon)
· pinch sea salt
· black pepper, to taste

METHOD

· Preheat your oven to I70°C/gas mark 4.
· Heat the oil in a medium frying pan, then add the onion and fry for 5 minutes. Add the aubergine pieces and fry for a further 5–8 minutes, until they turn a golden colour. Mix in the soy sauce and the sundried tomatoes, the herbs and the chilli flakes, and cook through.
· Slice the French bread or crusty rolls down the middle and lightly butter the bread. Wrap in baking foil and warm in the oven for 10 minutes.
· Spoon the aubergine mixture onto the bread, then crumble the feta cheese over the aubergine, followed by a squeeze of lemon juice. Season to taste with a small pinch of sea salt and a grind of black pepper. Serve hot.

POPCORN

Freshly popped corn is a favourite snack from my childhood. I can still remember the anticipation of waiting for the corn to start popping. It felt like a lifetime and, just when I thought it wasn't going to work, pop pop pop, it would go crazy! The gentle smell of popped corn would fill the kitchen. I like to eat it the classic American way with a little melted butter drizzled over the top, but I have included a sweet option here too. It's the perfect snack to eat when you're watching a movie at home.

SERVES 2-4

INGREDIENTS

To pop the corn:
· I teaspoon sunflower, vegetable or olive oil
· 160g popping corn

Buttery option:
· 3 tablespoons salted butter

Sweet option:
· 3 tablespoons salted butter
· 3 tablespoons soft brown sugar
· 3 tablespoons golden syrup or maple syrup

METHOD

· Take a large, heavy-bottomed saucepan with a lid (a see-through lid is best so you can see how the corn is popping).
· Put the oil in the pan over a medium heat. Once the oil is hot (near smoking point), tip in the popcorn kernels and immediately put the lid on the pan, so you don't let the heat out. Shake the pan gently so that the corn kernels don't get a chance to burn on the bottom of the pan.
· Wait until you hear the corn start to pop — it's only a short wait, so keep shaking the pan often so that the corn moves around and doesn't burn. When you hear the popping really slow down, take the pan off the heat and set it aside for a minute. Then tip the popped corn into a large mixing bowl. Mix together well with your preferred topping — and eat immediately.

· Buttery option: Melt the butter in a small saucepan and drizzle it over your popped corn. Mix well.

· Sweet option: Melt the butter in small saucepan, stir in the soft brown sugar and golden syrup until all melted together. Pour the topping over your popped corn and mix well to coat it.

DELUXE EGG MAYO

I used to love it when Mum made egg mayonnaise, because I could wipe any leftovers from the bowl with a piece of soft fresh buttered bread. So it has remained a favourite for me. I like this served in a soft seeded roll or as a generous filling for a toasted bagel. And I also love it as an open-faced sandwich just spread on a piece of toast, with a thin slice of fresh tomato on top.

MAKES 4–6 SANDWICHES, depending how much filling you like to stuff in!

INGREDIENTS

- 6 large, free-range eggs, hard-boiled
- I tablespoon finely chopped red onion or spring onions
- I stick celery, trimmed and finely chopped
- 4 heaped tablespoons mayonnaise
- I heaped teaspoon Dijon mustard (wholegrain or fine grain)
- I teaspoon cucumber relish (optional)
- sea salt and black pepper, to taste

METHOD

- Remove the shells from the hard-boiled eggs and, in a medium mixing bowl, mash the eggs with a fork.
- Mix in the chopped onion and celery. Then dollop in the mayonnaise, mustard and cucumber relish (if using) and mix together well. Season to taste with sea salt and black pepper.

HALLOUMI BBQ SKEWERS

These skewers are so quick and tasty. Grilled halloumi cheese is great with just about anything but it really comes to life with this tangy BBQ sauce. I like to have these served with steamed rice or new potatoes.

SERVES 4

INGREDIENTS

- ½ quantity BBQ Sauce (see p. 168)
- 2 small or medium onions or 8 small shallots
- 2 red peppers
- 2 courgettes
- 200g halloumi cheese

- 8 presoaked wooden skewers

METHOD

- Make the BBQ sauce, reducing the quantity by half.
- Peel the onions and chop into quarters (if using shallots, just peel). Remove the seeds from the peppers and discard, and cut into 8 pieces. Next, cut the courgettes and halloumi cheese into 8 pieces.
- Prepare the skewers by alternating the chunks of halloumi with the peppers, onions or shallots and courgettes; 2 pieces of each ingredient per skewer. Brush the prepared skewers with a generous amount of the BBQ sauce on all sides.
- To cook, place the skewers under a medium-hot grill for about 10–12 minutes, turning often until cooked and golden.
- Alternatively you can cook them in the oven at 180°C/gas mark 4 for 10–12 minutes. Or place them on a preheated barbecue.

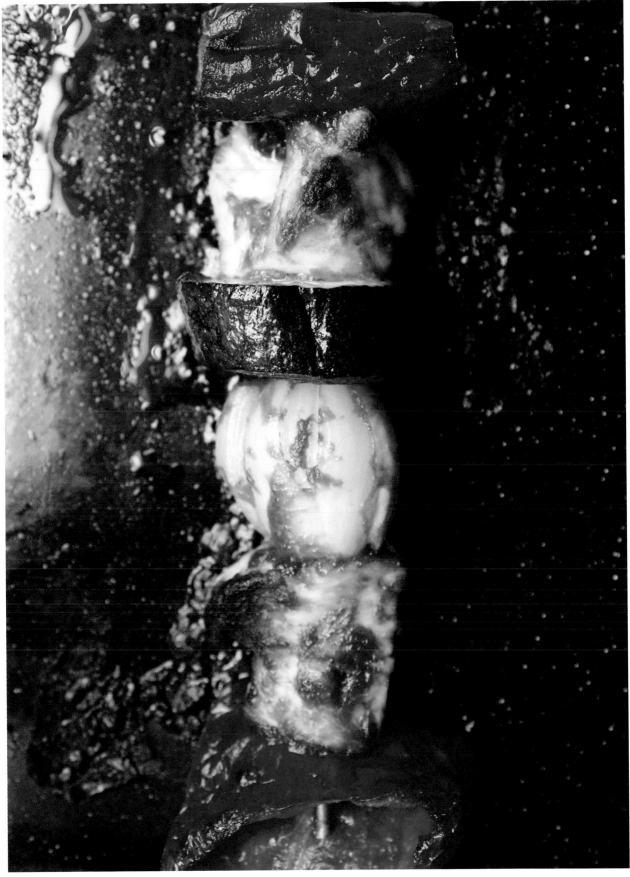

GUACAMOLE

This is a dip that my mum loved to make and it remains one of my favourites. I adore it — it's bright and satisfying and quick to make. It's more than just a dip to serve with tortilla chips or carrot sticks — I also find it irresistible spooned alongside a sandwich or onto a burrito, or dolloped onto a salad of mixed lettuce leaves. It's also tasty spread on top of a veggie burger. If you like coriander, then a tablespoon of the chopped herb stirred in works well too.

SERVES 2

INGREDIENTS

- 2 hass avocados, halved and stones removed
- I medium ripe tomato, finely chopped
- I small red chilli, deseeded and finely chopped, or 2 tablespoons chopped medium heat jalapeños (from a jar) or dash Tabasco sauce
- I clove garlic, finely chopped
- juice of 2 limes (approx. 3 tablespoons)
- pinch sea salt and freshly ground black pepper

METHOD

- Scoop the avocado flesh out of the halves and put in a medium mixing bowl. Mash well with a fork and then stir in the chopped tomato, chilli (or jalapeño or Tabasco), garlic and lime juice. Season with sea salt and freshly ground black pepper to taste.

JALAPEÑO TOSTADA

This is such a tasty snack and so quick and simple to make. The recipe is inspired by the cheese tostadas we used to eat at a family-favourite Mexican restaurant when I was growing up. I often make these for a super-quick supper and eat them with an Avocado Salad (p.84) on the side.

SERVES 1

INGREDIENTS

· 1 corn or flour tortilla (approx. 20cm)
· 6 slices cheese, such as Red Leicester, mature Cheddar or goat's Cheddar (approx. 80g)
· 2 tablespoons chopped jalapeños (from a jar) or green chillies

METHOD

· Preheat the grill to medium high. Line a baking tray with greaseproof or parchment paper.
· Place the tortilla on the baking tray. Lay the cheese on top of the tortilla, leaving a 1cm border around the outer edge of the tortilla so that when the cheese goes under the grill it melts up to, but not over, the edge.
· Sprinkle the jalapeños (or chillies) over the cheese. Now place your tostada under the grill for a couple of minutes, until the cheese is bubbly and fully melted. Serve immediately.

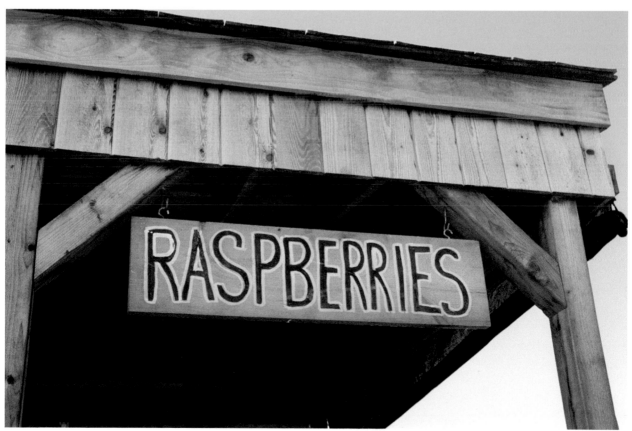

SOUPS, SALADS AND STARTERS

ROASTED BUTTERNUT SQUASH AND ROSEMARY SOUP

Roasting the butternut squash and the rosemary together first adds a luxurious aromatic twist to this delicious soup.

SERVES 4

INGREDIENTS

· I butternut squash
· 2 tablespoons light olive oil, plus more for drizzling over the squash
· 2 large sprigs fresh rosemary
· 2 medium onions, finely chopped
· 2 sticks celery, trimmed and chopped
· I medium carrot, chopped
· pinch (¼ teaspoon) chilli flakes (optional)
· 800ml vegetable stock
· sea salt and black pepper, to taste
· 2 tablespoons crème fraîche or soured cream, plus more for serving (optional)

METHOD

· Preheat your oven to I70°C/gas mark 3.
· Slice the butternut squash in half, scoop out and discard the seeds and put both halves on a baking tray. Drizzle with a little olive oil and lay the rosemary sprigs in the hollow of each half of squash. Bake for 45 minutes. Now allow the squash to cool slightly, discard the woody sprigs but keep the leaves from the rosemary, then peel off the outer skin of the squash and chop the flesh into cubes.
· In a large saucepan sauté the onions, celery and carrot in the oil for about 5 minutes. Mix in the squash pieces and the pinch of chilli flakes, if using, and then pour in the vegetable stock. Allow this to simmer gently for I5 minutes. Season with freshly ground black pepper and a little sea salt to taste.
· When the mixture has cooled slightly, ladle it into a blender (or use a handheld blender). Mix in the crème fraîche or soured cream and whizz until smooth, about I5 seconds.
· Pour the soup back into the saucepan, heat through and serve topped with a dollop of crème fraîche or some Herby Croutons (see p.I60).

HEARTY QUINOA AND WHITE BEAN SOUP

This is a warming and very satisfying soup. I like to use quinoa because it's a really nutritious superfood that provides a great source of protein. The grainy texture helps to make this soup filling enough to provide a meal in itself.

SERVES APPROX. 6

INGREDIENTS

- 4 tablespoons light olive oil
- 2 medium onions, finely chopped
- 2 large carrots, finely chopped
- 2 sticks celery, trimmed and diced
- 400g tin white or cannellini beans
- 2 cloves garlic, finely chopped
- 400g tin chopped tomatoes
- 1.5 litres vegetable stock
- 60g quinoa
- 4 tablespoons chopped fresh parsley
- 1 tablespoon chopped fresh oregano, rosemary or thyme
- 1 bay leaf
- sea salt and black pepper, to taste

METHOD

- Heat the oil in a large, heavy-bottomed saucepan over a medium heat. Add the onions, carrots and celery and sauté for 5 minutes. Then add the beans and garlic and sauté for a further couple of minutes.
- Stir in the chopped tomatoes and vegetable stock, and simmer for 20 minutes.
- Finally, add the quinoa, parsley, oregano or other herbs and the bay leaf, and cook for 12–15 minutes, to allow the quinoa to cook through. Season with sea salt and black pepper to taste.

FARM STALL

OP
all week

PRODUCE
- EGGS
- VEGETABLES
- FRUIT
- APPLE JUICE
- POTATOES
- PRESERVES

EASY-PEASY SOUP

This soup is a colourful vibrant green. It is really quick to make and uses frozen peas, so is a great option when you're running low on fresh green vegetables, and yet the end result is a wonderfully tasty sweet pea soup. Lovely served hot with crusty buttered bread.

SERVES 4

INGREDIENTS

· 2 tablespoons vegetable oil
· I leek, trimmed, washed and finely chopped
· 2 medium onions, finely chopped
· 3 cloves garlic, finely chopped
· 2 medium potatoes, cut into small cubes
· 600g bag frozen peas
· 900ml vegetable stock
· I teaspoon dried mixed herbs, or I tablespoon chopped fresh parsley
· 150g crème fraîche
· black pepper, to taste

METHOD

· In a medium-large heavy-bottomed saucepan heat the oil, then add the leek, onions and garlic and gently fry them for about 5 minutes. Add the cubes of potatoes and the frozen peas, stir well and fry for about 2 minutes. Now pour in the vegetable stock and add the herbs. Stir well and then leave to simmer gently for 15 minutes.
· Leave this to cool just a little and then blend, using either a pitcher blender or a hand blender in the saucepan. Stir in the crème fraîche and a pinch of black pepper.

LIP-SMACKING MINESTRONE

I have always been a big fan of minestrone — the chunky texture and the hearty ingredients are so flavoursome and comforting. You can have it as a lunch or starter, but it's filling enough to make a light supper too. I make a big batch and eat it throughout the week.

It's also a very versatile dish; you can mix and match vegetables that are in season and therefore make it slightly different according to what you have in your fridge and what you are in the mood for. The pasta is an optional extra as you might prefer a lighter soup. I find that kids love the little stars of the stellette soup pasta. And if basil is in season it's nice to add a handful of roughly broken-up basil leaves to the soup in the last 10 minutes of cooking.

This soup is great on its own topped with lots of grated Parmesan, or with garlic bread or a sandwich to dip in, or with buttered fresh bread… Yum, this is making me hungry!

SERVES 4–6

INGREDIENTS

- 3 tablespoons light olive oil
- I medium onion, finely chopped
- I medium leek, trimmed, washed and finely chopped
- 2 stalks celery, trimmed and finely chopped
- 2 medium to large carrots, finely chopped
- 400g tin chopped tomatoes
- 2 cloves garlic, finely chopped
- I litre vegetable stock
- 150g green cabbage, grated or finely chopped
- I tablespoon chopped fresh parsley
- 2 teaspoons chopped fresh oregano
- I bay leaf
- I tablespoon tomato purée
- 4 tablespoons frozen peas or peeled broad beans
- 50g dried small macaroni, or 50g stellette soup pasta or spaghetti, broken up (optional)
- sea salt and black pepper, to taste
- grated Parmesan or other hard cheese, to serve

METHOD

- Heat the olive oil in a large, heavy-bottomed saucepan, then add the chopped onion, leek, celery and carrots, stirring well, and cook for a couple of minutes on a medium heat, to allow the flavours of the vegetables to release.
- Stir in the chopped tomatoes and the garlic, then cover and simmer for 15 minutes, checking and stirring often. Pour in the vegetable stock, then add the cabbage, herbs and the bay leaf, and mix in the tomato purée. Bring to the boil and let it simmer for 15 minutes.
- Add the frozen peas, or broad beans, and pasta and continue to simmer gently for a further 15 minutes. Add more stock if it's too thick. Taste, and season with sea salt (only if it needs it as the stock may be salty enough) and ground black pepper to taste. Ladle generously into soup bowls and sprinkle with grated Parmesan cheese.

MUST-HAVE CREAMY TOMATO SOUP

One of my favourite meals has always been a bowl of hot tomato soup eaten with a grilled cheese sandwich; it's like medicine to me — and pretty much guaranteed to cheer me up.

SERVES 4

INGREDIENTS

· 3 tablespoons light olive oil
· 3 medium onions, finely chopped
· 2 sticks celery, trimmed and chopped
· 2 cloves garlic, finely chopped
· 6 ripe tomatoes, blanched, skinned and chopped
· 800g tinned tomatoes
· 200ml vegetable stock
· I tablespoon tomato purée
· I tablespoon each chopped fresh rosemary leaves
  and sage, or 25g roughly chopped basil
· 200ml single cream or soya cream or crème fraîche
· sea salt and black pepper, to taste

METHOD

· Heat the oil in a medium to large, heavy-bottomed saucepan. Add the onions and celery and sauté for 10 minutes, then stir in the garlic and continue to sauté for a couple more minutes. Stir in the chopped fresh tomatoes.
· Mix in the tinned tomatoes, vegetable stock and the tomato purée. Let this mixture simmer slowly for 12–15 minutes. Then mix in the herbs and take off the heat.
· Stir in the cream (or crème fraîche). Now season with a large pinch of sea salt and some freshly ground black pepper to taste. Heat through until hot enough to serve.

LIGHTNING LENTIL SOUP

As the title implies, this is a quick soup that delivers on flavour and is also very satisfying. I find it's a great way to get the kids to eat lentils without complaining. This is best served hot with some garlic bread for dipping.

SERVES 4

INGREDIENTS

· 2 tablespoons light olive oil
· 3 medium onions, finely chopped
· 2 medium carrots, finely chopped
· 2 sticks celery, trimmed and finely chopped
· 400g tin green lentils, preferably biona organic green lentils, drained
· ¼ teaspoon ground cumin
· 1½ teaspoons tomato purée
· 600ml vegetable stock
· freshly ground black pepper, to taste
· pinch chilli flakes (optional)

METHOD

· Gently heat the oil in a medium to large heavy-bottomed saucepan and then add the chopped onions, carrots and celery. Sauté for 3–4 minutes to allow the vegetables to start cooking and release their flavours. Tip in the drained tin of lentils and mix together well.
· Stir in the cumin and tomato purée and heat through. Pour in the vegetable stock and allow the soup to simmer gently for 15 minutes.
· Let it cool slightly, then transfer the soup to a blender and whizz for about 15 seconds (or use a hand blender in the saucepan).
· Transfer the blitzed soup back to the saucepan and heat it up again. Add a fresh grinding of black pepper to taste, and a pinch of chilli flakes if you want an extra kick.
· If you prefer a chunky soup, then do not blend.

LEEK, COURGETTE AND BUTTER BEAN SOUP

I love the subtle blend of flavours in this soup. If I don't have courgettes, I sometimes use green beans instead and that works really well too.

SERVES APPROX. 4

INGREDIENTS

- 2 tablespoons vegetable oil
- 2 medium leeks, trimmed, washed and finely chopped
- 2 courgettes (approx. 400g), chopped small
- I stick celery, trimmed and finely chopped
- 400g tin butter beans
- 800ml vegetable stock
- ½ teaspoon dried mixed herbs

METHOD

- Heat the vegetable oil in a medium to large saucepan and gently fry the leeks until they are soft and golden, which should take about 7 minutes. Stir in the courgettes, celery and butter beans, and fry for another 4 minutes or so.
- Pour in the vegetable stock and add the herbs, mixing well. Cover and simmer gently for I5 minutes.
- Allow the soup to cool slightly and then whizz in a blender, or use a hand blender in the saucepan (or you can serve this chunky, depending on your preference). Pour the soup back into saucepan to reheat and then pour into bowls. It's good served topped with the Herby Croutons (see p.I60).

AUBERGINE WRAPS

These wraps work well as a dinner party dish — either as a starter or as a main course with side dishes, such as warm potato salad or sautéed leeks with courgettes, alongside. You can assemble them beforehand and then bake them when your guests arrive, making for a more relaxing evening for you.

SERVES 4 (4 wraps per person)

INGREDIENTS

- 2 medium/large aubergines
- 2 tablespoons sunflower oil or light olive oil
- 1 tablespoon dried mixed herbs
- 400g spinach
- 16 sundried tomato pieces marinated in olive oil
- 3 tablespoons pine nuts, lightly toasted in a hot frying pan (no oil needed)
- 150g mature Cheddar, cut into 16 slices
- pinch sea salt
- black pepper, to taste

METHOD

- Preheat your oven to 180°C/gas mark 4. You will need a large non-stick baking tray.
- Cut the woody top off each aubergine, and discard. Slice each aubergine lengthways into 8 pieces (16 in all) about 1.5cm thick.
- Mix the oil and the herbs together in a small bowl or cup. Lightly brush each slice of aubergine with the herby oil on both sides. Heat a large frying pan to medium hot and lay as many pieces of the aubergine in the pan as will comfortably fit. Fry each side until golden brown and softened, which should be about 3 minutes on each side. When all the slices are cooked, set them aside.
- Wash the spinach well in cold running water, then wilt it in a medium saucepan (using just the water that is clinging to the leaves) and drain off the excess liquid.
- Now, start to assemble each wrap by taking 1 slice of the cooked aubergine and placing a little of the wilted spinach on one half. Then lay a piece of sundried tomato on top, sprinkle with a few toasted pine nuts, and top with a slice of Cheddar. Fold the aubergine over to form the wrap, then place it on a large non-stick baking tray.
- Repeat this until all 16 wraps are assembled and placed side by side on the baking tray. Sprinkle with a pinch of sea salt and a grind of fresh black pepper.
- Bake in the oven for 15 minutes, until the cheese has melted and is bubbling, and serve immediately.

CORN FRITTERS

These fritters make a great starter or lunch. They work really well with various different sauces and dips, such as a spoonful of guacamole on the side (see p.53 for a recipe), or with sweet chilli dipping sauce or even a yogurt and cucumber dip. I like to use fresh chilli, but a pinch of dried chilli flakes works well too. When I am making these for kids, or friends that don't like spice, I just leave out the chilli.

SERVES 4 (Makes about 12 x 8cm fritters)

INGREDIENTS

· 120g plain or spelt flour
· ½ teaspoon baking powder
· 2 large, free-range eggs, beaten
· 90ml semi-skimmed milk
· 300g sweetcorn, cut fresh off the cob (or frozen sweetcorn, thawed, or tinned sweetcorn, drained)
· 1 clove garlic, finely chopped
· 1 red chilli, deseeded and finely chopped (optional)
· 2 spring onions, trimmed and finely chopped
· 1 tablespoon chopped fresh parsley or coriander
· sea salt and black pepper, to taste
· approx. ¾ tablespoon vegetable oil, for shallow frying

For the dipping sauce:
· 6 tablespoons plain yogurt
· ½ small fresh red chilli, finely chopped
· 1 tablespoon finely chopped fresh parsley or coriander
· 1 tablespoon chilli jam or sweet chilli sauce
· ½ teaspoon freshly squeezed lemon juice

METHOD

· In a medium to large mixing bowl mix together the flour and baking powder, then gradually stir in the beaten eggs and milk. Mix well to form a smooth batter.
· Stir in the sweetcorn, garlic, chilli (if using), spring onions and herbs, and mix the ingredients well so that they are coated in the batter. Season to taste.
· Heat the vegetable oil in a large non-stick frying pan until it is hot. You can test this by dropping a tiny bit of the batter into the pan — you should hear it sizzle when it hits the pan.
· Spoon in a tablespoon of the mixture for each fritter, leaving space between them so that they don't stick together (you may need to do this in batches). Pat each fritter down a bit so it's flatter and easy to cook on both sides. Fry until golden brown and then turn them over to brown the other side. This should take about 2 minutes each side. Repeat this process until all the mixture has been cooked.
· Serve immediately, or wrap the fritters in baking foil and keep warm in a low oven until they're all done.
· To make the dipping sauce, just mix all the ingredients together in a small bowl.

AVOCADO SALAD

You will need to use ripe avocados for this salad – give them a little squeeze to check that they give a bit. If they are too hard, do not use them yet, but wait a few days to allow them to ripen. This is a great salad to have with the Black Bean, Sweetcorn and Feta Tacos on p.120.

SERVES 4

INGREDIENTS

For the dressing:
- 4 tablespoons extra-virgin olive oil
- 2 tablespoons freshly squeezed lemon or lime juice (from approx. I lemon/lime)
- sea salt and black pepper, to taste

For the salad:
- 2 ripe hass avocados
- 2 spring onions, trimmed and finely chopped
- 2 ripe tomatoes, chopped small
- I fresh red chilli (medium heat), deseeded and finely chopped, or 6 slices of jalapeños in brine (from a jar), drained (optional)
- 2 tablespoons pine nuts, toasted in a hot frying pan (no oil)
- handful basil leaves, roughly chopped

METHOD

- Make the dressing first. In a cup or small bowl, whisk together the olive oil, lemon or lime juice, a little sea salt and a grind of black pepper. Set this aside.
- Cut the avocados in half, remove the stones, peel, and slice the flesh into a salad bowl, then add the chopped spring onions and tomatoes, the chilli (or jalapeños), if using, the toasted pine nuts and chopped fresh basil. Drizzle the dressing over the salad, and toss well. Check the seasoning and add an extra pinch of sea salt and another grind of freshly ground black pepper if you feel it needs more.

SPROUTING CARROT SALAD

My mum would often rustle up a chef's salad in a huge wooden bowl, making it up as she went along with whatever ingredients were to hand. I still do that today when I can't think of what else to prepare, and there's not much that can't – or doesn't – get thrown in. From the virtuous to the wonderfully sumptuous, there's a salad to go with any occasion. The best bit is you can always remind yourself you're being healthy, and with this one … you are.

SERVES 2

INGREDIENTS

· 100g alfalfa sprouts, washed and dried
· 2 medium carrots, grated
· 2 baby gem lettuces, chopped

For the dressing:
· 2 tablespoons extra-virgin olive oil
· I tablespoon balsamic or white wine vinegar
· I tablespoon freshly squeezed lemon juice
· pinch sea salt
· freshly ground black pepper, to taste

METHOD

· Combine all the salad ingredients in a medium salad bowl or mixing bowl.
· Drizzle the olive oil, vinegar and lemon juice over the salad, and toss together well. Season with a pinch of sea salt and some black pepper to taste.

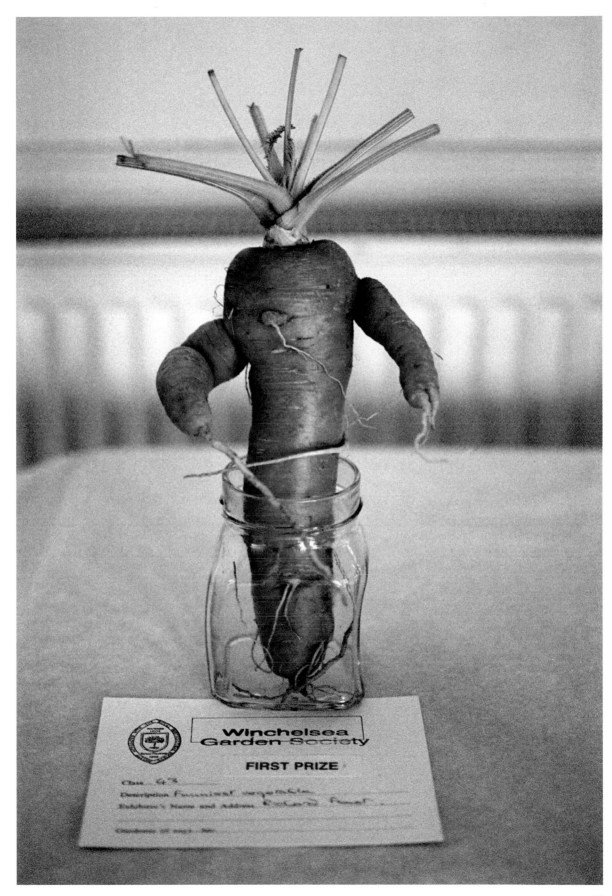

WATERCRESS, RADISH AND FETA SALAD

Salads seem to play a part in pretty much every meal we have during the summer months. I grew up thinking that huge, fresh salads, tossed in a large wooden salad bowl with my mum's home-made dressing, were the norm. Then one day, as a young teenager, I went to my best friend's house for supper and her mum asked if I would like salad. I was amazed when I was served a slice of cucumber, a slice of tomato and a piece of lettuce with salad cream poured over the top! This one goes really well with the One-pot Mushroom Rice on p.126.

SERVES 2

INGREDIENTS

· 100g watercress, washed and dried
· 8 radishes, thinly sliced
· 80g feta cheese

For the dressing:
· 2 tablespoons extra-virgin olive oil
· I tablespoon freshly squeezed lemon juice
· sea salt and black pepper, to taste

METHOD

· First, remove any tough woody stems from your watercress.
· Then toss the watercress and radishes into a medium salad bowl and crumble in the feta cheese.
· Drizzle the olive oil and lemon juice over the salad and then season with a pinch of sea salt and a couple of grinds of black pepper.
· Toss together and serve immediately.

LENTIL AND FETA SALAD

Puy lentils work well in this salad because they have a tender texture and hold their shape when cooked. This salad is a tangy, tasty way of getting lentils into your diet – ensuring a good supply of protein and fibre.

SERVES 2

INGREDIENTS

- 200g dried puy lentils
- 500ml vegetable stock
- 5 spring onions, trimmed and finely chopped, or ¼ medium red onion, finely chopped
- 2 medium ripe tomatoes, chopped small
- 3 tablespoons chopped fresh basil or parsley
- 2 tablespoons freshly squeezed lemon juice (from approx. ½ lemon)
- 2 tablespoons extra-virgin olive oil
- 100g feta cheese, crumbled
- pinch sea salt
- black pepper, to taste

METHOD

- Put the lentils into a sieve and rinse them under cold running water, then drain. Transfer them to a medium saucepan and pour the vegetable stock over them. Bring to the boil and gently simmer for about 15-20 minutes, until the stock has boiled off (or the lentils are al dente).
- Pour the lentils back into the sieve again and give them a quick rinse under running water. Drain well and place them into a medium mixing or salad bowl.
- Stir in the chopped spring onions, tomatoes and basil or parsley. Mix in the lemon juice and olive oil. Crumble in the feta cheese and mix it all together. Season with a pinch of sea salt and some freshly ground black pepper to taste, and serve. This salad is best served at room temperature.

HALLOUMI AND ROASTED RED PEPPER SALAD

The sweetness of the roasted red peppers alongside the saltiness of the pan-fried halloumi is a vibrant taste combination I really enjoy.

SERVES 2

INGREDIENTS

For the dressing:
- 2 tablespoons extra-virgin olive oil
- I tablespoon red onion or shallot, finely chopped
- I tablespoon freshly squeezed lemon juice (from approx. ½ lemon)

For the salad:
- 2 fresh red peppers (approx. 200g), preferably romano red peppers (or buy a jar of ready-roasted red peppers)
- I pack halloumi cheese (approx. 200–240g)
- 2 tablespoons light olive oil
- I ripe tomato, chopped
- I teaspoon chopped fresh thyme (optional)
- I teaspoon chopped fresh mint
- I tablespoon chopped parsley
- small pinch sea salt
- black pepper, to taste

METHOD

- Make your dressing first: in a cup or small bowl, mix together the extra-virgin olive oil, finely chopped red onion or shallot and lemon juice.
- To roast the red peppers, preheat the grill to medium/high. Place the whole red peppers on a baking tray and then under the grill. Allow the skin to blacken, and then turn the peppers so that eventually the whole of each pepper has blackened skin. Turn off the grill and leave the peppers to cool slightly. When they have cooled enough for you to be able to handle them, peel away all the skin from the red flesh of the peppers, and discard the skin. Keep the red flesh of the peppers, but discard the stalks and the seeds. Finally, slice the peppers into thin strips.
- Unwrap the halloumi cheese and pat it dry with some kitchen paper. Cut it into 8 equal slices.
- Cook the halloumi just before you are ready to serve the salad. To do this, heat the light olive oil in a medium to large frying pan over a medium heat. When the pan is hot, add the slices of cheese to the pan and cook both sides until lightly browned.
- To assemble the salad, arrange the roasted red peppers and the tomato, chopped, equally on your serving plates. Lay the slices of fried halloumi on top.
- Sprinkle the chopped herbs over the cheese. Drizzle the dressing over the salad and season with a small pinch of sea salt and some freshly ground black pepper to taste.

BALSAMIC ROASTED SHALLOT SALAD

I love shallots: their oniony, garlic flavour goes perfectly with the sweetness of the balsamic vinegar when they are baked together, and they are the ideal bite size. This salad looks beautiful too.

SERVES 2

INGREDIENTS

- 6 shallots (approx. 180g), peeled
- 1 tablespoon balsamic vinegar
- 1 tablespoon light olive oil
- pinch sea salt
- 6 cherry tomatoes
- 10 walnuts (approx. 40g), broken into pieces
- 80g mixed salad leaves, e.g. rocket, watercress, baby spinach

For the dressing:
- ½ teaspoon mustard, preferably Dijon
- 1 teaspoon balsamic vinegar
- 3 teaspoons extra-virgin olive oil
- small pinch sea salt

METHOD

- Preheat your oven to 180°C/gas mark 4.
- Line a baking tray with baking foil and arrange the peeled shallots on top. Drizzle the balsamic vinegar and light olive oil over the shallots, coating the shallots well in the mix. Sprinkle over the salt.
- Bake the shallots for 30 minutes, checking every 10 minutes or so and mixing them around in their dressing. After 15 minutes, add the cherry tomatoes to the tray to bake for the remaining 15 minutes. Take the tray out of the oven and leave to cool to room temperature.
- Meanwhile, in a small, heavy-bottomed frying pan (no need to add oil) toast the walnuts for a couple of minutes on a medium heat, shaking often so they don't burn.
- Make the dressing by combining the mustard, vinegar and extra-virgin olive oil in a medium salad bowl. Add a small pinch of sea salt and whisk with a fork. Add the salad leaves to the bowl and gently toss the leaves so they are lightly coated in dressing.
- Arrange the shallots, tomatoes and toasted walnuts on top of the dressed salad leaves. Ready to serve!

MIXED LEAVES, BLUE CHEESE AND RED GRAPE SALAD

This salad makes a great supper party starter and is really quick to prepare. It never ceases to surprise me just how good blue cheese tastes with red grapes and a simple vinaigrette. One of those odd but brilliant bits of food alchemy!

SERVES 2

INGREDIENTS

· 2 baby gem lettuces
· handful mixed leaves, such as watercress, baby spinach and rocket
· 60g blue cheese, such as Dolcelatte or Danish blue, cubed or crumbled
· 8 red grapes, halved
· 10 walnuts, broken in half and lightly toasted in a frying pan (no oil needed)

For the dressing:
· 4 teaspoons extra-virgin olive oil
· 1 teaspoon freshly squeezed lemon juice
· 1 teaspoon white wine vinegar or similar
· pinch sea salt and black pepper, to taste

METHOD

· Wash and dry the lettuce and mixed leaves and place them in a medium salad or mixing bowl, then scatter the blue cheese, red grapes and walnuts over the top. Drizzle with the olive oil, lemon and white wine vinegar, and toss well. Season with a pinch of sea salt and some freshly ground black pepper and it's ready to serve.

SUPER QUINOA SALAD

Quinoa is a brilliant form of protein and a 'superfood', so I am always keen to come up with different recipes that incorporate it. As I love salads and dressings, this is one of my preferred ways of eating quinoa. Served with a piece of toast spread with hummous, it's perfect for lunch.

SERVES 2

INGREDIENTS

- 60g quinoa
- 2 spring onions, trimmed and finely chopped
- I ripe tomato, finely chopped
- I carrot, very thinly sliced or chopped small
- 2 tablespoons finely chopped fresh parsley

For the dressing:
- I teaspoon Dijon mustard (fine grain)
- juice of I lemon (approx. 2 tablespoons)
- 3 tablespoons extra-virgin olive oil
- pinch sea salt
- black pepper, to taste

METHOD

- Simmer the quinoa in water (approx. 200ml), checking the cooking instructions on the packet. Drain, set aside and leave to cool. Then transfer the quinoa, spring onions, chopped tomato, sliced carrot and parsley into a medium salad bowl or mixing bowl. Toss together well.
- In a small bowl or cup, using a fork, whisk together the mustard, lemon juice and olive oil. Season with a small pinch of salt and some freshly ground black pepper. Drizzle the dressing over the quinoa and vegetables, mix together well and serve.

NEW POTATO AND ASPARAGUS SALAD WITH MUSTARD DRESSING

This salad works really well served with the quiche on p.114. But it also makes a great addition to a summer barbecue or picnic. I love to make it when asparagus is in season in the early summer months.

SERVES 2

INGREDIENTS

- 500g new potatoes, washed
- 125g fine asparagus, trimmed

For the dressing:
- 2 tablespoons extra-virgin olive oil
- 1 tablespoon balsamic vinegar
- 2 teaspoons Dijon mustard (wholegrain or fine grain)
- pinch sea salt and freshly ground black pepper

METHOD

- Place the new potatoes in a medium to large saucepan, cover with water and bring to the boil over a high heat. Then reduce the heat to medium so that the potatoes simmer gently for 12–15 minutes, depending on their size. Test them with a fork to ensure they are definitely cooked through. Then drain them of all water and set aside to cool.
- Simmer the asparagus in boiling water until just cooked, which should be about 2–4 minutes depending on the thickness of the asparagus. Drain and cut in half. Leave to cool.
- To make the dressing, mix together the olive oil, balsamic vinegar and Dijon mustard, and season with a pinch of sea salt and some black pepper to taste.
- Place the new potatoes and asparagus in a medium salad bowl, pour the dressing over and gently mix together well. Ready to serve.

MAINS

CHEESE AND AUBERGINE OVEN BAKE

This dish is wonderful as it comes but sometimes, just for a change, I like to vary the recipe. A pinch of chilli flakes added to the tomato sauce provides a great kick, and 100g veggie mince cooked into the tomato sauce adds substantial 'bite' to the meal. Feel free to play around with it too. This is good served with sautéed leeks and a leafy salad or steamed green beans.

SERVES 4

INGREDIENTS

- 4 tablespoons light olive oil
- I medium onion, finely chopped
- 2 cloves garlic, finely chopped
- 400g tin chopped tomatoes
- I tablespoon tomato purée
- I tablespoon dried mixed herbs, plus a pinch
- pinch sea salt
- sea salt and black pepper, to taste
- 2 medium aubergines sliced widthways into discs Icm thick
- I tablespoon soy sauce
- 100g soft goat's cheese or chopped mozzarella
- 120g goat's Cheddar or mature Cheddar, grated
- handful fresh basil leaves (if available), roughly chopped (approx. 50g)

METHOD

- Preheat the oven to 180°C/gas mark 4.
- First make the tomato sauce. In a medium heavy-bottomed saucepan heat 2 tablespoons of the olive oil and gently sauté the chopped onion until softened and slightly golden brown in colour — about 8 minutes. Then stir in the garlic and tinned tomatoes, tomato purée, mixed herbs, a small pinch of sea salt and some black pepper to taste. Simmer gently for 20 minutes, stirring often, until the sauce has thickened. Set aside.
- In a small bowl combine the remaining 2 tablespoons of olive oil, the soy sauce and a pinch of mixed herbs. Lightly brush both sides of each aubergine slice with the olive oil mixture. Sauté the slices in batches in a large non-stick frying pan, cooking for 3–4 minutes until golden brown.
- Spread a third of the tomato sauce over the bottom of a medium baking dish. On top of this place a layer of aubergine slices and then spoon I teaspoon of tomato sauce over each aubergine disc. Scatter with crumbled pieces of the soft goat's cheese followed by a layer of aubergine. Spoon the remaining tomato sauce over the aubergine slices and, finally, scatter the basil leaves and grated Cheddar on top.
- Bake for 15–20 minutes, until the tomato sauce and cheese are bubbling and the cheese is lightly brown on top.

MEXICAN BEAN TORTILLA

This recipe has a medley of flavours, colours and textures — and it makes a bright and satisfying meal in itself.

SERVES 2-4 (I or 2 tortillas per person)

INGREDIENTS

- 2 tablespoons cooking oil
- I medium red onion, halved and thinly sliced
- 6 chestnut or cup mushrooms, thinly sliced
- ½ red pepper, preferably romano, chopped into bite-sized pieces
- I red chilli, deseeded and finely chopped, or ½ teaspoon chilli flakes (optional — leave out if you do not want the heat)
- 415g tin refried beans, or 400g tin pinto beans, drained
- 4 corn or flour tortillas (approx. 20cm each in diameter)
- 2 ripe hass avocados
- 2 limes
- 100g salad leaves (e.g. lettuce or baby spinach), washed, dried and roughly chopped
- I tablespoon extra-virgin olive oil, for drizzling over the lettuce leaves
- sea salt and freshly ground black pepper, to taste
- 4 tablespoons soured cream or crème fraîche
- 2 tablespoons chopped coriander (optional)

METHOD

- Preheat your oven to 180°C/gas mark 4 (for heating the tortillas).
- In a large frying pan sauté the red onion in the cooking oil for 3 minutes, then add the mushrooms, red pepper and chilli and sauté for a further 5 minutes, until nearly cooked through.
- Mix in the tin of beans and stir well, until nice and hot, which will take about 5 minutes.
- Prepare the tortillas by wrapping them in aluminium foil and heating in the oven for about 10 minutes, until they're nice and hot.
- Halve the avocados, remove the stones, then scoop out the fruit with a dessertspoon and cut into bite-sized cubes. Put these into a medium mixing bowl and squeeze over the juice of one of your limes and sprinkle with a pinch of sea salt, then mix well.
- In a separate salad bowl, mix the lettuce or baby spinach leaves with a drizzle (I tablespoon) of olive oil and the juice of half the remaining lime. Season with sea salt and black pepper to taste.
- To assemble: take the warm tortillas and place on each serving plate. Spoon on the bean mix and spread it across the base of each tortilla, about 2cm thick. Top with the salad, and then the diced avocado. Dollop a spoonful of soured cream on top and follow with a grind of freshly ground black pepper. Garnish with some chopped coriander (if you like it). Eat immediately!

CHEESY QUICHE

This is my version of one of my mum's recipes that I love to pass on to friends and family – it's a sharing recipe! The secret to making the quiche puff up and rise, is to cook it at a high oven heat. I like to serve it with crushed buttered new potatoes and steamed vegetables or a leafy green salad. Leftover quiche can be kept in the fridge for a few days, so it's great warmed up for lunches or sliced and packed up for picnics.

SERVES 6

INGREDIENTS

- 300g shortcrust pastry dough, home-made (see p.166) or shop-bought
- flour, for dusting work surface
- 2 tablespoons vegetable or cooking oil
- 6 medium onions, finely chopped (I like to use 3 red onions and 3 white onions)
- 1 tablespoon chopped mixed fresh herbs (such as parsley, thyme, etc.)
- 6 large, free-range eggs
- 500ml milk
- 250g mature Cheddar cheese, grated
- freshly ground black pepper, to taste

METHOD

- Preheat your oven to 180°C/gas mark 4.
- Roll out the pastry on a clean, lightly floured surface to about 30cm diameter, 3mm thick, and then line a metal pie dish (24–26cm) with the pastry. To keep the crust from becoming too soggy once the filling is poured in you will need to pre-bake (blind bake) the pastry. To do this, line the pastry in the pie dish with greaseproof paper or baking parchment and then fill it with just enough dried beans or rice to cover the base. Bake for 10 minutes. Allow the beans or rice to cool, then carefully remove them and the greaseproof paper and set aside (the beans or rice can be stored in a container to reuse for blind baking in the future). Put the pie dish back in the oven to cook for a further 5 minutes. Take it out and set aside.
- Now turn up the oven to 200°C/gas mark 6.
- In a medium frying pan sauté the onions in the oil for 10–15 minutes, until they soften and turn golden, then mix in the herbs. Take it off the heat and allow them to cool slightly.
- In a large mixing bowl beat the eggs and whisk in the milk, so that the eggs are light and have air bubbles. Stir in the grated cheese and fried onions, and season with black pepper.
- Pour the mixture into the pastry case and bake for 30–35 minutes, until the filling has risen and is well browned on top. The centre should have a spring to the touch when you push it gently in the middle.

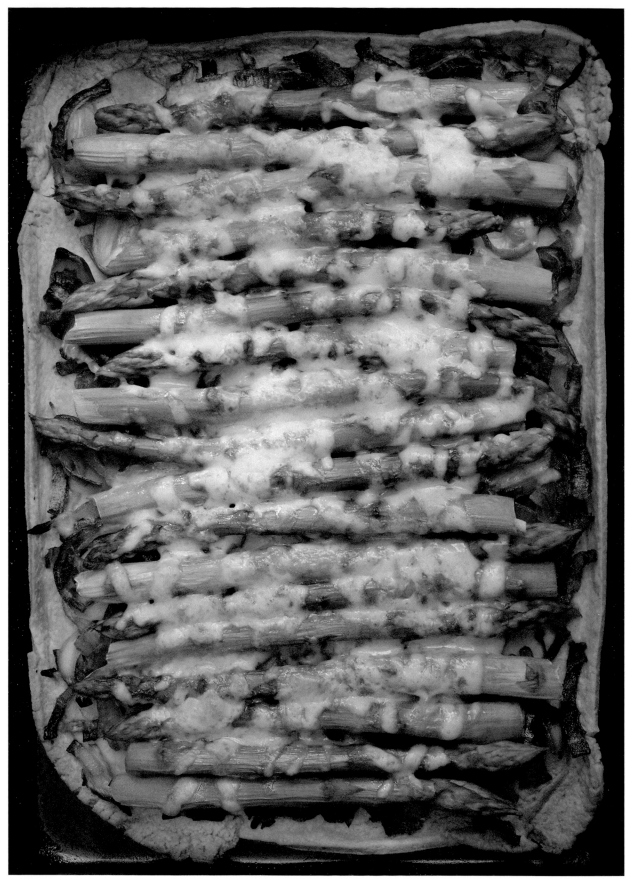

ASPARAGUS SUMMER TART

The slow-cooked, sweet red onions add an extra dimension to this asparagus tart. Making it for friends is great because you can prepare it before your guests arrive and then pop it in the oven 15 minutes before you are ready to eat. I like to serve this with a simple green leaf salad with a lemon and olive oil dressing.

SERVES 4

INGREDIENTS

- 250g cream cheese pastry (see p.164) or shop-bought shortcrust pastry
- 2 tablespoons vegetable cooking oil
- 4 medium red onions, thinly sliced
- large bunch fresh asparagus (approx. 450g)
- 150g good melting cheese, such as Gruyère, taleggio, applewood smoked Cheddar or goat's Cheddar, cubed or grated
- freshly ground black pepper

METHOD

- Preheat your oven to 170°C/gas mark 3.
- Roll out your pastry to about 3mm thick and lay it in a baking tray (approx. 32 x 20cm) to fit the edges. To blind bake your pastry case, lay parchment or greaseproof paper onto your rolled pastry, and then tip your baking beans or rice on top to gently weigh it down. Bake it for 10 minutes, then remove the paper and beans and bake again for about 5 minutes, until the pastry is lightly golden but not fully cooked.
- For the filling: heat the oil in a medium heavy-bottomed frying pan, and then gently fry the onions on a medium/low heat until they are soft and caramelised (about 15 minutes).
- To prepare the asparagus, clean all the spears under cold water and then snap or cut off just the woody ends (you can discard these). Boil in just enough water to cover them, for 2–3 minutes, depending on thickness. They should be slightly undercooked, as they will finish cooking in the oven.
- Spread the caramelised onions evenly over the base of your pre-baked pastry case and then arrange the asparagus over the onions. Sprinkle the cheese on top and season with freshly ground black pepper.
- Bake the tart in the oven for about 15 minutes, or until the pastry is golden and the cheese is bubbling hot and turning golden brown. Cut into portions, and serve.

BUTTER BEAN GRAVY STEW

This stew has a luxurious rich gravy sauce and goes well with steamed long-grain rice, or over mashed potato with some steamed seasonal vegetables and cauliflower cheese on the side. As a variation, I sometimes like to add a glug (about 100ml) of red wine just before adding the stock, and then I let it simmer gently for 5 minutes to allow the alcohol to burn off. And a pinch of red chilli flakes adds a nice hot kick if you're in the mood.

The veggie burger needs to be a firm one that's made from soya protein, not soft potato or vegetables, otherwise it won't hold its shape when cooking.

SERVES 2

INGREDIENTS

- 2 tablespoons vegetable oil
- 2 medium leeks (approx. 200g), trimmed, washed and chopped — or 2 medium onions, chopped
- 8 button mushrooms, thinly sliced
- I tablespoon soy sauce
- 400g tin butter beans, drained
- I veggie burger, cooked and chopped into cubes (optional)
- I tablespoon chopped fresh parsley, or 2 teaspoons dried mixed herbs
- I½ tablespoons cornflour
- 300ml vegetable stock, cooled
- sea salt and black pepper, to taste

METHOD

- In a large saucepan or a large frying pan with deep sides, heat the oil and gently sauté the leeks or onions for 5–8 minutes, until they are soft and starting to turn golden. Stir in the mushrooms and soy sauce, and fry for a further 5 minutes. Add the chilli (if using). Then stir in the butter beans, the cooked and cubed veggie burger and herbs, and allow them to heat through for a couple of minutes.
- Then mix together the cornflour and cold vegetable stock and pour this into the stew, stirring all the time to ensure it doesn't go lumpy. Simmer gently for IO minutes, stirring often, until the mixture has thickened to a creamy consistency. Check the seasoning and add a little salt and pepper if required.
- And now it's ready to serve. It's good with a spoonful of crème fraîche or soured cream and freshly ground black pepper on top.

SPINACH, LEEK AND COURGETTE FRITTATA

This makes a quick and nutritious meal. I sometimes have it for brunch too, but then I would leave out the courgettes. It's great served with potato salad or cooked new potatoes tossed in butter and herbs.

SERVES 2

INGREDIENTS

- 200g fresh spinach
- 2 tablespoons cooking oil
- I leek, trimmed, washed and finely chopped
- I medium onion, finely chopped
- I medium courgette, trimmed and cut into small cubes
- I teaspoon chopped fresh oregano, or I teaspoon dried herbs
- I teaspoon chopped fresh thyme, or dried
- 5 large, free-range eggs
- I tablespoon butter, for frying
- 100g feta cheese
- sea salt and freshly ground black pepper, to taste

METHOD

- Wash the fresh spinach leaves thoroughly and then wilt them in a medium saucepan on a medium heat. The spinach releases a lot of liquid when cooking, so you don't need to add any water. Once the leaves have wilted, take off the heat and allow to cool slightly. When you can handle the spinach, squeeze out the excess liquid, and chop up the leaves. Set aside.
- Now heat the sunflower oil in a medium frying pan. Add the leek and onion, courgette and herbs and sauté them for about 8 minutes on a medium heat (so that you can hear the sizzling) until they are turning golden. Add the chopped cooked spinach, heat through and then remove from the pan onto a dish or plate while you prepare the eggs.
- Preheat the grill to medium setting. Crack the eggs into a mixing bowl and beat them together.
- Then, using a medium frying pan, melt the butter over a medium to high heat. Pour in the eggs. Scatter your previously cooked vegetable over the cooking eggs and crumble the feta cheese evenly on top. Add some freshly ground black pepper and a pinch of salt to taste. Cook for a couple of minutes, so that the eggs are turning golden on the base of the pan.
- Then place the pan under the grill, keeping the handle turned away from the grill, so that it does not overheat. Cook through till the eggs have set on top too.
- Gently slide the frittata onto a serving plate to cut into pieces. I like this served warm, but it can be eaten at room temperature too.

BLACK BEAN, SWEETCORN AND FETA TACOS

I've always loved tacos but this is a little deviation from how I usually make them, to include the sweetcorn. My mum loved Mexican food and she also loved sweetcorn, eating it from the cob when it was in season. I think it adds a lovely crunchy texture to this particular taco combination. The added bonus is that these are quick and easy to make.

SERVES 2 (2 tacos per person)

INGREDIENTS

- 3 tablespoons vegetable cooking oil
- I medium onion, finely chopped
- 400g tin black beans
- 3 cloves garlic, finely chopped
- 4 slices jalapeño (from a jar), chopped, or ½ teaspoon chilli flakes, or ½ teaspoon finely chopped fresh red chilli
- pinch sea salt, or to taste
- ½ teaspoon ground cumin
- 100g sweetcorn, fresh from the cob or frozen or tinned
- 4 taco shells
- 100g feta cheese, crumbled
- juice of I lime

METHOD

- Preheat your oven to 180°C/gas mark 4.
- Heat the oil in a medium frying pan and sauté the chopped onion on a medium heat for 5 minutes. Drain and rinse the black beans in a sieve, and then mix them into the onion in the pan. Add the garlic, and the jalapeño or chilli, followed by the sea salt and the cumin, and heat for 5 minutes until cooked through.
- To cook the sweetcorn, place it in a small saucepan with boiling water (from the kettle) and simmer for a couple of minutes until hot. Then drain.
- In the meantime, wrap the taco shells in baking foil and put them in the oven to heat up for 5–10 minutes.
- When the taco shells are well heated, take them out of the oven, then spoon the bean mix evenly between the 4 tacos, top with the cooked sweetcorn and, finally, sprinkle the crumbled feta over the top. Finish off with a little squeeze of lime juice, and serve hot.

BUTTERED COURGETTE AND CHEESY POLENTA

Polenta is basically Italian cornmeal porridge… it can be a delicious alternative to mashed potato because it's got a great, unctuous consistency and can be flavoured for a more intense taste. This way of cooking it gives it a savoury edge, which acts as a base for the subtle courgette topping. You could substitute the courgettes with mushrooms, or chuck in a handful of sliced mushrooms to cook along with them.

SERVES 4

INGREDIENTS

For the buttered courgettes:
· 2 tablespoons butter
· 3 courgettes, trimmed and cut into long thin strips
· 2 cloves garlic, finely chopped
· 2 tablespoons chopped fresh parsley
· sea salt and black pepper, to taste
· squeeze of lemon juice (½ lemon)

For the polenta:
· 600ml vegetable stock
· 600ml milk
· 300g quick-cook polenta
· 100g butter
· 75g Parmesan or mature Cheddar, grated

METHOD

· Heat the butter in a medium frying pan and add the courgettes, mixing to ensure they are well coated in the butter. Stir in the garlic and parsley and sauté for 5–8 minutes, or until the courgettes are tender. Season with sea salt and pepper to taste, and then squeeze a little lemon juice over the courgettes and combine well.

· In a large saucepan, heat the stock and milk together until almost boiling, then gradually whisk in the polenta. Keep stirring until the mixture has thickened, although you still want it to be soft, like the consistency of porridge. Add a little more milk or water, if necessary. Stir in the butter and cheese and season to taste with black pepper.

· Spoon the polenta onto plates and lay the prepared courgettes on top. Serve hot.

LEEK AND PEA RISOTTO

This silky, creamy risotto looks so good with the subtle green of the leeks and peas, and it has wonderfully smooth flavours. You can play around with the vegetables you use, for instance substituting 6 shallots for the leeks.

SERVES 4

INGREDIENTS

- 3 tablespoons light olive oil
- I tablespoon butter
- 2 medium leeks, finely chopped
- I medium onion, finely chopped
- I stick celery, finely chopped
- 250g risotto rice
- 2 cloves garlic, finely chopped
- 2 teaspoons chopped fresh thyme or parsley
- 150ml dry white wine (optional)
- I litre heated vegetable stock, plus more stock or boiled water if needed
- 200g frozen or fresh shelled peas, or chopped green beans
- sea salt and black pepper, to taste
- 4 tablespoons grated Parmesan, plus more for serving

METHOD

- Melt the oil and butter together in a large heavy-bottomed saucepan on a medium heat. Stir in the chopped leeks, onion and celery and then slow-cook gently for about 15 minutes, to allow the leeks and onions to sweat and go translucent, rather than brown. Add the rice and garlic and mix well, coating the rice in the oil, and let it cook, stirring often for a couple of minutes, to allow the rice to heat through, not brown. Now stir in the herbs and the white wine (if using).
- Add a couple of ladlefuls of the heated stock (about 200ml), enough to cover the rice. Mix well, and allow to simmer gently, stirring frequently, until the stock is nearly absorbed, but do not let the rice cook too quickly. Gradually add more stock and keep stirring, until all of it has been absorbed; do not allow the risotto to dry out, you want a thick soupy consistency. Stir in the peas halfway through cooking the rice, after about 7 minutes. After about 15 minutes the rice should be cooked through but still al dente. If you run out of stock and the rice is not cooked yet, then use some extra stock or boiled water to finish off — but be careful not to let it overcook and become soggy or stodgy.
- Season with black pepper — if you're using powdered or cubed vegetable stock it may not need any extra salt. Once it's cooked, remove from the heat and stir in the Parmesan. Mix well and allow it to sit for I or 2 minutes. Then serve immediately, with extra Parmesan and black pepper to taste.

ONE-POT MUSHROOM RICE

Taking the time to slow-cook the onions and mushrooms before adding the rice gives it much more flavour. And it doesn't create much washing-up! My best friend from school says that she can't get her son to eat mushrooms except for this dish that he requests specially.

SERVES 4

INGREDIENTS

- **3 tablespoons light olive oil**
- **3 medium red onions, finely chopped**
- **200g button, chestnut or large flat-cap mushrooms, finely chopped**
- **2 teaspoons dried mixed herbs**
- **1 tablespoon soy sauce**
- **200g long-grain rice**
- **500ml vegetable stock**
- **4 tablespoons frozen peas**
- **sea salt and black pepper, to taste**
- **grated Parmesan or mature Cheddar, or crème fraîche, to serve (optional)**

METHOD

- **Gently heat the olive oil in a large saucepan, stir in the onions and sauté them for 8 minutes. Next, stir in the mushrooms, mixed herbs and soy sauce, and gently sauté them for a further 10–12 minutes, until the natural juices from the mushrooms have evaporated and the mushrooms have started to turn golden brown.**
- **Add the rice and stir well for a minute so the rice is well coated. Pour in the vegetable stock and leave to simmer gently for about 15 minutes, or until the rice has cooked through but has not had a chance to turn too soft.**
- **Mix in the frozen peas and stir well, heating through, and season with sea salt and black pepper to taste. Serve topped with grated cheese or a spoonful of crème fraîche, if you want.**

SAGE AND ONION ROAST

This is the roast terrine I like to cook for Sunday lunch, served with all the traditional trimmings of roast vegetables, steamed greens and Yorkshire puddings. And leftovers can be reheated and served midweek with gravy, steamed green beans and a generous spoonful of horseradish sauce on the side.

SERVES 4

INGREDIENTS

- 3 tablespoons light olive oil
- 2 medium onions, finely chopped
- 2 sticks celery, finely chopped
- 40g pine nuts, lightly toasted in a frying pan (no oil needed)
- 40g walnuts, chopped
- 100g peeled and cooked chestnuts, chopped
- 3 tablespoons chopped fresh sage
- 100g veggie mince
- 125g breadcrumbs
- 200ml vegetable stock
- 3 large, free-range eggs, beaten
- sea salt and black pepper, to taste

METHOD

- Preheat the oven to 190°C/gas mark 5. Line a 23cm loaf tin (about 10cm deep) with greaseproof paper or baking parchment.
- In a large frying pan, heat the olive oil and gently sauté the chopped onions and celery for about 5–10 minutes. Stir in the pine nuts, walnuts, chestnuts, chopped sage and the veggie mince. Sauté for a minute or two until heated through. Now add the breadcrumbs and cook for another 8–10 minutes.
- Stir in the vegetable stock and cook through for a couple of minutes. Transfer the mixture to a large mixing bowl and allow it to cool for a couple of minutes. Then stir in the beaten eggs, season with salt and plenty of black pepper and mix together well.
- Spoon the mixture into the lined loaf tin and push it down evenly.
- Bake the terrine in the middle of the oven for 30 minutes. Then take it out of the oven and turn it upside down onto a non-stick baking tray, peeling away the baking paper. Put it back in the oven to bake for a further 30 minutes, until the outside is crisp and golden. Slice and serve with the Red Onion Gravy on p.171.

WINTER WARMER HOTPOT

I make this a lot, because it is packed with fresh veg and easy to put together — by allowing it to slow-cook in the oven it comes out full of flavour. I like it served with a dollop of crème fraîche or soured cream on top and some freshly ground black pepper. A meal-in-one dish.

SERVES 4

INGREDIENTS

- 3 large potatoes (or 6 medium), cut widthways into thin round slices
- 3 medium onions, halved then cut widthways into thin slices
- 2 medium carrots, cut into cubes
- 250g green beans, trimmed and chopped
- 420g tin butter beans, drained
- 3 vegetarian sausages (or burgers), cooked and chopped into chunky bite-sized pieces (optional)
- 2 tablespoons chopped fresh parsley, or 2 teaspoons dried mixed herbs
- 800ml vegetable stock (allowed to cool), mixed with 1 tablespoon cornflour
- 2 tablespoons light olive oil, for drizzling on top
- black pepper, to taste

METHOD

- Preheat your oven to 180°C/gas mark 4.
- Take half of the potato slices and arrange them in the bottom of a casserole or baking dish (about 29cm). Layer all of the onion slices over them, then scatter the carrots and green beans over the onion, followed by the butter beans and then the sausage or burger pieces (if using). Sprinkle in the herbs and finish with a final layer of the remaining potato slices.
- Now carefully pour in the vegetable stock, which should come to about 1cm below the final (top) layer of potato. Drizzle with the olive oil, grind over some black pepper and cover the dish with baking foil.
- Place the dish on the middle shelf in the oven. Leave to cook for 1 hour 45 minutes, then take off the baking foil, dot the potatoes with butter or olive oil and cook for a further 15 minutes, until the top layer of potatoes is golden and slightly crisp.

SHEPHERD'S PIE

This is a classic comfort meal, because it has the indulgence of the creamy mashed potato topping that goes perfectly with the juicy gravy below. I like it with a squeeze of ketchup on the side! It's also versatile — you can swap the green beans for frozen peas, you can play around with the herbs, and a glug of red wine in the gravy is usually a welcome extra. If you have any left over, this is such a good dish to reheat on demand throughout the week. I like this served with lightly buttered spinach.

SERVES 6

INGREDIENTS

For the topping:
- 900g floury potatoes (e.g. King Edward), peeled and chopped into large cubes
- 60g butter
- 150ml milk
- 1 teaspoon mustard, preferably Dijon (fine or wholegrain)
- pinch sea salt and black pepper, to taste
- 75g mature Cheddar, grated (optional)

For the filling:
- 2 tablespoons vegetable or light olive oil
- 1 large onion, finely chopped
- 1 garlic clove, finely chopped
- 1 stick celery, trimmed and finely chopped
- 1 medium carrot, finely chopped
- 250g greens beans, chopped, or 150g frozen peas
- 6 button mushrooms, chopped into small pieces
- 200g veggie mince
- 2 tablespoons cornflour
- 750ml vegetable stock, cooled
- 2 tablespoons tamari or soy sauce
- 1 tablespoon tomato purée
- 1 tablespoon chopped herbs (fresh parsley and oregano if possible), or 1 teaspoon dried mixed herbs
- 100ml red wine (optional)

METHOD

- Preheat your oven to 180°C/gas mark 4.
- Place the peeled potato chunks into a large saucepan, cover with water and bring to the boil. Boil for 15–20 minutes, until they are tender, then drain.
- Mash the potatoes well and return the pan to a low heat. Stir in the butter, milk and mustard and whisk with a fork to make a light, fluffy and smooth mash. Season with a pinch of sea salt and black pepper.
- To make the filling, heat the oil in a large heavy-bottomed pan and gently fry the onion for 5 minutes. Stir in the garlic, celery, carrot, green beans, mushrooms, and finally the veggie mince, mix well and cook for a further 2–3 minutes.
- Spoon the cornflour into a measuring jug and slowly stir in the cooled vegetable stock. Pour this over the vegetables and veggie mince, stirring well, then increase the heat to bring it to a gentle simmer. Add the tamari or soy sauce and the tomato purée and herbs (and also the red wine, if using). Let it gently simmer for 15–20 minutes.
- Spoon the filling into a large ovenproof dish. Top with large spoonfuls of the mashed potato, gently smoothing it over with a fork so the potato covers the filling. Sprinkle with the grated cheese and a little more black pepper to taste.
- Bake in the oven for 30 minutes. The top should be golden brown and the filling will be bubbling.

WHITE SPAGHETTI SAUCE

This is a fast and simple pasta sauce. It is very tasty and quite indulgent. But it is white! And I have an obsessional need to have something green on my plate to make a meal feel complete. With that in mind, I love this served with a watercress or rocket salad, or steamed green vegetables such as spinach or runner beans.

SERVES 4

INGREDIENTS

- 1 tablespoon light olive oil
- 250g crème fraîche
- 2 tablespoons milk
- generous grinding fresh black pepper, or to taste
- 350g dried spaghetti or linguine (or other dried pasta of your choice)
- 100g Parmesan, grated, plus more to serve
- pinch sea salt, or to taste

METHOD

- Gently heat the oil in a large frying pan. Add the crème fraîche and milk, and stir well until heated through. Grind in some black pepper to taste, take the pan off the heat and set it aside.
- Now cook the pasta in a large, heavy-bottomed saucepan of boiling salted water (check the packet for cooking time — about 8–10 minutes and the pasta should be cooked but still firm to the bite, not soggy).
- Once the pasta is cooked, drain it in a colander or large sieve, then add it to the white sauce in the frying pan and mix together so all of the pasta is coated in the sauce, heating it through again on a medium to low heat. Stir in the grated Parmesan and serve hot with extra Parmesan, some more ground black pepper and a pinch of sea salt on top according to your taste. Best eaten immediately.

MAC CHEESE WITH CRISPY TOPPING

I love macaroni and cheese with a blob of tomato ketchup on the side and served with nothing more than some cooked frozen peas. It's so satisfying when you've had a busy day and are in need of proper comfort food.

SERVES 4

INGREDIENTS

· 400g dried macaroni pasta
· 30g butter
· 4 tablespoons plain flour
· 450ml milk
· I teaspoon Dijon mustard
· 200g mature Cheddar cheese, grated
· 50g Parmesan cheese (or similar), grated
· black pepper, to taste

For the crispy topping:
· 60g breadcrumbs
· 3 tablespoons finely grated Parmesan cheese
· I tablespoon finely chopped fresh parsley
· I tablespoon finely chopped mixed pumpkin and
  sesame seeds (optional)

METHOD

· Cook the macaroni in a large pan of boiling salted water. Stir it from time to time to make sure the pasta doesn't stick together or to the bottom of the pan. Undercook the pasta by a couple of minutes (check the packet for cooking time and deduct 2 minutes), so it is not quite cooked through, as it will go in the oven to finish later. Drain the pasta in a colander and set it aside while you make the topping.
· Preheat your oven to 190°C/gas mark 5.
· Make the topping by mixing together the breadcrumbs, Parmesan, fresh parsley and finely chopped seeds in a medium bowl.
· To make the cheese sauce, melt the butter in a large, heavy-bottomed saucepan and then stir in the flour, mixing very well for about 20 seconds to make a paste. On a gentle heat gradually add the milk, stirring constantly, to give a nice, thick, creamy sauce. Stir in the mustard. Take the sauce off the heat and then stir in the grated cheese, mixing well until it is melted and the sauce is completely smooth — if it seems too thick, add a little more milk. Season with black pepper to taste.
· Now add the cooked pasta to the pan and mix the pasta and sauce together so it is all coated.
· Transfer the macaroni cheese to a baking dish, spreading it out evenly. Sprinkle the breadcrumb mix over the top, then bake for 20–25 minutes until the sauce is bubbling and the topping has turned golden and crisp.

MUSHROOM AND LEEK LASAGNE

This is a good dinner party dish that can be assembled in advance and then put in the oven when your guests have arrived, to cook for 40 minutes or so before serving.

SERVES 4–6

INGREDIENTS

· 30g dried porcini mushrooms
· 2 tablespoons vegetable oil
· 3 medium leeks, trimmed, washed and finely chopped
· 1 medium onion, finely chopped
· 250g button mushrooms, thinly sliced
· 2 teaspoons chopped fresh thyme
· 2 large, free-range eggs
· 200g feta cheese, crumbled
· 250g (12 sheets) lasagne pasta sheets
· 100g soft goat's cheese or cream cheese
· 200g mature Cheddar or goat's Cheddar, grated
· freshly ground black pepper, to taste

For the sauce:
· 2 tablespoons cooking oil
· 3 tablespoons plain or spelt flour
· 200ml porcini stock (reserved from soaking the dried mushrooms, see method)
· 500ml milk
· sea salt and black pepper, to taste

METHOD

· Preheat the oven to 180°C/gas mark 4.
· Rehydrate the dried porcini mushrooms in a bowl of warm water (about 15 minutes), or as per the packet instructions.
· Meanwhile, in a large frying pan heat the 2 tablespoons of vegetable oil, add the chopped leeks and onion and sauté for 6–8 minutes until they are soft and golden. Then stir in the sliced button mushrooms and sauté until tender, which should be about 5 minutes.
· Once the porcini mushrooms are rehydrated, set aside 200ml of the stock to make the sauce, then drain the porcini mushrooms of the rest of the liquid. Mix them along with the thyme into the large frying pan. Sauté for 5–10 minutes, until cooked through. Season with salt and black pepper to taste, and set aside.
· To make the porcini sauce, gently heat the 2 tablespoons of cooking oil in a medium saucepan, then stir in the flour and heat together. Gradually add the reserved porcini stock and mix together well to avoid lumps. Slowly add the milk, stirring constantly, and then simmer very gently and stir often until the sauce has thickened to a creamy consistency that coats the spoon. Season with a pinch of sea salt and some freshly ground black pepper to taste. Take the sauce off the heat and set it aside.
· Now for the final component. In a small mixing bowl, beat together the 2 eggs and mix in the crumbled feta cheese.

· Time to assemble the lasagne. Spread the base
of a medium baking dish (about 26cm) with a third
of the sauce mix. Cover this evenly with a layer
of the lasagne sheets, and spread a third of the
mushroom and leek mix over the sheets. Now
spoon all of the egg and feta mix evenly over this,
followed by another layer of lasagne sheets. Top
with another third of the porcini sauce and then a
third of the mushroom and leek mix. Crumble the
goat's cheese over the mushroom and leek mix
and lay another layer of lasagne sheets on top.
Pour over the remaining sauce and the remaining
mushroom and leek mix, and finally sprinkle evenly
with the grated Cheddar.

· Grind some black pepper to taste over the lasagne

and then put it into the oven for 30–40 minutes,
until it is golden and bubbling hot. If cooking the
lasagne from chilled, allow an extra 5–10 minutes to
heat through.

· Remove from the oven and serve. This lasagne is
great eaten with a fresh chopped salad, or seasonal
steamed vegetables.

CAULIFLOWER CHEESE

Cauliflower cheese is an old classic and a firm favourite. It's a good way of getting kids to eat veg too – I sometimes add broccoli or a handful of frozen peas. I sometimes serve it with baked beans. My preference is always for mature Cheddar, as it adds real punch, and I sometimes like to use wholemeal flour as it gives the sauce a bit of extra texture.

SERVES 2 as a main course, or 4 as a side dish

INGREDIENTS

- 1 medium head cauliflower, approx. 600g
- 2 tablespoons cooking oil or butter
- 3 tablespoons plain or spelt flour
- 500ml milk
- 1 teaspoon Dijon mustard
- 200g mature Cheddar, grated
- 50g Parmesan, grated
- black pepper, to taste

METHOD

- Remove the outer leaves of the cauliflower and discard, then cut the cauliflower into quarters. Place the 4 pieces into a steamer and steam the cauliflower for 10 minutes, or until it is just tender (it will continue to cook in the oven). Arrange the cauliflower pieces in a medium baking dish and set it aside.
- Preheat your oven to 180°C/gas mark 4.
- In the meantime you can start on the sauce. In a medium saucepan gently heat the cooking oil or butter, stir in the flour for about 30 seconds, then add a fifth of the milk. Stir well until it thickens then add another fifth of the milk and stir again until it is thickened — and continue in this way until all the milk is used up. Add the mustard and stir it in well. Now take the sauce off the heat and tip in most of the cheese, holding back 1 tablespoon of the Cheddar and 1 tablespoon of the Parmesan, which you will use to sprinkle on top before you put the dish in the oven. Mix well until the cheese is completely melted. Add a few grinds of black pepper to taste.
- Pour the cheese sauce over the cauliflower pieces in the baking dish. Sprinkle the remaining grated cheese over the top.
- Put in the oven and bake for 12–15 minutes, until the top is golden brown and the sauce is bubbling hot.

YUMMY SPICY RICE NOODLES

This noodle dish is totally moreish. It's spicy, peanutty and irresistible as either lunch or dinner. If I have friends round for dinner I like to serve the Corn Fritters (see p.82) as a starter and then the Coconut Rice Pudding with Chocolate Sauce (see p.206) for dessert. The main thing is to not to overcook the rice noodles as they will get heated again when you warm all the ingredients together at the end.

SERVES 4–6

INGREDIENTS

For the sauce:
- 3 tablespoons crunchy peanut butter
- 2 tablespoons chilli jam, or 4 tablespoons sweet chilli sauce
- 300ml heated vegetable stock
- I tablespoon toasted sesame oil
- 2 tablespoons soy or tamari sauce
- 6 tablespoons coconut milk

For the noodles and vegetables:
- 3 bundles flat rice noodles (approx. 400g)
- 2 tablespoons toasted sesame oil, plus more for the noodles
- 125g baby sweetcorn, cut into pieces, or 150g tinned or frozen sweetcorn
- 2 medium carrots, thinly sliced
- I medium red onion, halved and thinly sliced
- 125g green beans, chopped
- 150g broccoli, broken into small florets
- 3 cloves garlic, finely chopped
- chopped peanuts and coriander, to serve (optional)

METHOD

- Put all your sauce ingredients into a mixing jug, and mix together well, so that the heated vegetable stock softens the ingredients together. Set aside while you prepare the vegetables.
- Cook the rice noodles following the packet instructions (but maybe a minute less than they suggest), then drain them in a colander and toss them in a little sesame oil to prevent them from sticking together. You do not want the noodles too soft, but still al dente, as they will be heated again in the vegetables and sauce at the end.
- To prepare the vegetables, heat the 2 tablespoons of sesame oil in a large frying pan with deep sides (or use a wok or big saucepan). Stir-fry all the vegetables together with the garlic for about 3 minutes on a medium to high heat, until the vegetables are just starting to soften slightly.
- Pour the sauce onto the vegetables in their pan and simmer gently for 4–5 minutes, until the vegetables are cooked through but still have a good bite to them and are not too soft.
- Now stir in the cooked rice noodles. Mix together well and heat through. I serve this hot, and sometimes garnished with chopped peanuts and chopped coriander.

COURGETTE AND LEMON SPAGHETTI

This recipe came about when I was scanning the contents of my kitchen cupboards and fridge, trying to find something I could whip up in less than half an hour that wouldn't create lots of dish-washing chaos. I like the sharpness of the feta combined with the freshness of the courgettes and the tanginess of the lemon. Also the flecks of herbs add an extra dimension that makes this dish burst with flavour.

SERVES 2

INGREDIENTS

· 200g dried spaghetti
· 3 tablespoons light olive oil, plus more for drizzling on drained spaghetti
· 2 courgettes, thinly sliced lengthways
· 3 cloves garlic, finely chopped
· 1½ teaspoons chopped fresh sage
· 1½ teaspoons chopped fresh rosemary
· 2 tablespoons grated Parmesan or pecorino cheese, plus more for serving (optional)
· 100g feta cheese, crumbled (optional)
· zest of ½ lemon
· sea salt and black pepper, to taste

METHOD

· First cook the spaghetti (check the packet for specific instructions) by bringing a large saucepan of water to the boil, adding a couple of large pinches of sea salt and then the spaghetti; it should take about 8–10 minutes to cook. Stir every so often so the strands of pasta don't stick together. When the pasta is just cooked (al dente), drain it in a colander, drizzle with a little olive oil and then mix to lightly coat the pasta and prevent the strands from sticking together. Set it aside.
· You can use the same saucepan to make your sauce. Pour in the 3 tablespoons of olive oil and bring to a medium heat, then add the courgettes and sauté for 4–5 minutes, before adding the garlic and herbs and mixing well. Sauté for a couple more minutes, to allow all the flavours to come together and the courgettes to cook through.
· Return the cooked spaghetti to the pan and heat through, then mix in the cheese and lemon zest, and season with a little sea salt (you may not need much as the feta cheese is salty) and a good grind of black pepper. Serve, with a little more grated cheese sprinkled over if you wish.

TOMATO AND RED WINE SAUCE

This is a really versatile sauce that can form the base for so many pasta dishes. You can add 80g of veggie mince to make it into an alternative Bolognese sauce. My eldest son likes to add a chopped red pepper when he is frying the onions as a variation too. Once you get the basic sauce right, you'll find your own variation that makes it personal to you.

SERVES 6

INGREDIENTS

- 3 tablespoons light olive oil
- 2 medium onions, finely chopped
- 4 cloves garlic, finely chopped
- 800g tinned chopped tomatoes
- 2 tablespoons tomato purée
- good glug red wine (approx. 80ml)
- 1 tablespoon dried mixed herbs, or 1 tablespoon chopped fresh oregano
- small handful fresh basil, if available (approx. 40g), plus more to serve
- freshly grated Parmesan, to serve

METHOD

- Heat the olive oil in a large deep-sided frying pan, and then add the chopped onions — you want to hear a nice sizzle as they cook. Gently sauté them for about 10 minutes, until they are caramelised, and then add the chopped garlic. Give it a good stir with a wooden spoon to make sure the garlic is well coated in olive oil, and cook for another minute.
- Add the chopped tomatoes and stir well, then mix in the tomato purée. Gently simmer for about 5 minutes. Then, as the sauce simmers, stir in the red wine and dried mixed herbs or fresh oregano.
- Gently cook for a further 15 minutes. Break up the basil and add that to the sauce too.
- Serve topped with a fresh basil leaf and some grated Parmesan.

BASICS AND SIDES

ROASTED ROSEMARY NEW POTATOES

If you do not have new potatoes, then other roasting potatoes can be used instead — just chop them into chunks and parboil, and follow the recipe in the same way. These are lovely served with Butter Bean Gravy Stew (p.118), or with the Sage and Onion Roast (p.130) and Red Onion Gravy (p.171), with some steamed green vegetables alongside.

SERVES 2

INGREDIENTS

- 500g new potatoes
- 3 tablespoons vegetable oil
- 5 sprigs rosemary
- pinch sea salt

METHOD

- Preheat the oven to 180°C/gas mark 4.
- Place the new potatoes in a medium to large saucepan, cover with water, bring to the boil and parboil for 5 minutes.
- Drain the water from the saucepan and set the potatoes aside.
- Pour the vegetable oil into a large baking tray and put in the oven to heat for a few minutes until it is sizzling hot.
- Take the tray out of the oven and add the sprigs of rosemary and the potatoes to the oil.
- Sprinkle a pinch of sea salt over the potatoes and mix everything together well. Place the tray back in the oven and roast the potatoes for 30 minutes.

HERBY CROUTONS

SERVES 4

INGREDIENTS

- 4 slices bread (you can use any variety — wholemeal, multigrain, spelt, white, etc.)
- 2 tablespoons light olive oil
- ½ teaspoon sea salt
- I tablespoon mixed herbs (dried or fresh)

METHOD

- Preheat the oven to 160°C/gas mark 3.
- Cut the bread into bite-sized cubes and place in a mixing bowl. Drizzle the olive oil and salt over the bread, followed by the herbs, and mix well so that the bread is lightly coated. Spread the coated cubes evenly on a baking tray and place in the oven. Cook until they are golden brown, which should be about 15 minutes.

PESTO SAUCE

SERVES 4

INGREDIENTS

- I clove garlic, finely chopped
- pinch sea salt
- large handful fresh basil leaves (approx. 90g), roughly chopped
- 50g pine nut kernels or walnuts, finely chopped
- 50g Parmesan, or similar hard cheese, finely grated
- 4 tablespoons extra-virgin olive oil

METHOD

- Grind the garlic with a pinch of salt and the basil leaves in a pestle and mortar. Add the pine nuts (or walnuts) and pound again into a paste. Turn out the ingredients into a small mixing bowl and stir in the finely grated Parmesan. Then finish by mixing in the olive oil so that the sauce has a gooey consistency.
- If you do not have a pestle and mortar, you can chop the garlic, basil and pine nut kernels together on a large chopping board and then turn out into the mixing bowl. Or you can blend all the ingredients together in a food processer fitted with a steel blade.

YORKSHIRE PUDDINGS

My husband taught me how to make Yorkshire puddings, and now I am hooked on them. I like to make them as individual puds, baked in a greaseproof muffin tin, but you can also bake as one large pudding in a deep-sided baking tray and then cut it into portions. As a child, my dad used to eat them as a sweet dessert — you follow the same recipe but finish off by pouring warm golden syrup over the top. Comfort food at its best.

SERVES 4 (2 puddings per person)

INGREDIENTS

· 100g plain or spelt flour
· pinch sea salt
· 2 large, free-range eggs
· 280ml milk
· 8 teaspoons cooking oil, for the muffin tin

METHOD

· Preheat your oven to 200°C/gas mark 6.
· Sift the flour into a medium-sized mixing bowl and add a pinch of salt. Crack the eggs in and whisk together with the flour, then gradually pour in the milk, stirring constantly. Beat all the ingredients together until the batter is the consistency of single cream. Leave this batter to rest in the fridge or a cool place for 30 minutes.
· Pour 1 teaspoon of oil into the base of each of 8 hollows in a greaseproof muffin tin. Put the muffin tin in the oven to heat the oil until it's very hot — almost smoking hot (about 5 minutes).
· Give the batter a quick mix and then pour it equally into each hollow of the tin (you should hear it sizzle and it should bubble). Return the tin to the oven and bake the puddings for 20–25 minutes, until they have risen and are deep golden brown. These are wonderful with the Sage and Onion Roast (see p.130), the Red Onion Gravy (see p.171) and horseradish sauce.

CREAM CHEESE PASTRY

My grandmother taught me how to make this, and I was intrigued to learn that you could make a pastry using cream cheese! It can get quite sticky so I think it's best done in a food processor, and it's important to chill the dough in the fridge once it's mixed to allow it to firm up. This is a wonderfully indulgent creamy pastry that works really well for quiches and pies.

MAKES 400G

INGREDIENTS

- 125g butter, softened to room temperature
- 125g cream cheese
- 200g plain or spelt flour

METHOD

- If using a food processor: Mix the butter, cream cheese and flour in the processor bowl until the dough comes together. Remove from the bowl and gather the dough into a firm ball, flatten it slightly, then wrap it in clingfilm and put in the fridge to chill for about 2 hours, or overnight.
- If mixing by hand: Beat together the butter and cream cheese in a mixing bowl, then add the flour and mix well until the ingredients come together. Using your hands, form the dough into a ball, then wrap in clingfilm and chill in the fridge — again, for about 2 hours, or overnight.
- This pastry can be kept frozen for up to 6 weeks. Take out and allow time to defrost before rolling out.

SHORTCRUST PIE PASTRY

I was about 14 when I first attempted to make my own pastry, and it turned out rock hard and inedible. That put me off for a while, but then I asked my grandmother for help, and tackled a couple of pastry recipes that, once she had taught me a few tips, were vast improvements. The main lessons seem to be: don't overwork the butter and flour, and try to keep the butter cool.

Making my own pastry still gives me a great sense of satisfaction. I must admit, though, if I'm rushing around, I do sometimes end up using the shop-bought pastry that is always on standby in my freezer.

This pastry is great for the Cheesy Quiche (see p.114), the Delicate Apple Tart (p.214) and the Asparagus Summer Tart (p.117).

MAKES APPROX. 500G

INGREDIENTS

- 300g plain or spelt flour
- 150g chilled salted butter, cut into cubes
- 1 large, free-range egg yolk
- approx. 4 tablespoons cold water

METHOD

- If making by hand: Measure the flour into a medium to large mixing bowl, and add the cubes of butter. Using your fingertips, lightly rub the cubes into the flour until the mixture has the texture of breadcrumbs and no large lumps are left.
- Tip in the egg yolk and mix with a cutlery knife until the pastry begins to come together. Then add the cold water gradually, 1 tablespoon at a time, just enough so that the mixture forms a dough. Do add another tablespoon of water if it needs more to combine.
- Knead the dough lightly, shape into a large ball (or 2 evenly sized balls if you're making a pie which requires both base and topping), wrap in clingfilm and chill in the fridge for at least 30 minutes, or overnight.

- If using a food processor: Blend the flour and butter until the mixture has the texture of breadcrumbs. With the motor running, slowly add the egg yolk and then the water through the funnel, until it all starts to bind together. Chill in the fridge as above. It can be kept frozen for up to 6 weeks.

VEGETABLE STOCK

Making your own stock means you get to control exactly what goes into it, and you can adapt it to your own personal taste. Home-made stock will keep for about 3 days in the fridge, and it also freezes well, so you can freeze it in batches and store for up to 3 or 4 months. It's really flavoursome in soups, risottos, gravies, hotpots and stews. But I also often use a powdered vegetable stock such as Marigold Swiss reduced-salt vegetable bouillon powder.

MAKES APPROX. 800ML

INGREDIENTS

- I tablespoon light olive oil
- I medium onion, cubed
- 2 medium leeks, trimmed, washed and cut into chunky cubes
- I medium or large carrot, cut into chunky cubes
- I stick celery, trimmed and chopped
- 800ml cold water
- 2 cloves garlic, crushed in their skins
- I5 black peppercorns
- 2 tomatoes, chopped in half (optional)
- 4 sprigs fresh parsley, roughly broken
- 2 bay leaves
- pinch sea salt

METHOD

- Pour the olive oil in to a large, heavy-bottomed saucepan over a medium heat. Add the onion, leeks, carrot and celery, and cook gently for 2–3 minutes to let the flavours release — do not brown the vegetables, but just let them 'sweat'.
- Add the cold water and bring to a simmer. Now add the garlic, peppercorns, tomatoes, parsley and bay leaves, mix well and cover the pan. Let the mixture simmer gently for I5–20 minutes.
- Take the pan off the heat, mix in a pinch of sea salt and allow the stock to cool slightly. Strain the stock through a sieve, keeping the liquid, and discard the vegetables (unless you have another use for them). You can use it straight away or leave it to cool and then store in the fridge or freezer.

BBQ SAUCE

SERVES 6–8

INGREDIENTS

· 500g tomato ketchup
· juice of I lemon
· 2 tablespoons balsamic vinegar or white wine vinegar
· 4 cloves garlic, finely chopped
· 3 tablespoons mustard, preferably French Dijon
· 4 tablespoons light olive oil or vegetable oil
· sea salt and black pepper, to taste

METHOD

· Mix all the ingredients together in a bowl.
· Either refrigerate for later use or pour the sauce into a large baking tray and add burgers, sausages or chunky-cut vegetables of your choice. Make sure they get well coated with the sauce. Then all you have to do is cook them on your barbecue or under the grill — and enjoy.

AUNTIE'S CARAWAY COLESLAW

My Aunt Louise's coleslaw recipe is tangy and a bit different. I love my Aunt Louise.

SERVES 4

INGREDIENTS

· 200g white cabbage, thinly sliced or grated
· 200g red cabbage, thinly sliced or grated (or use 400g white cabbage if you don't have any red)
· I medium carrot, grated
· 2 teaspoons caraway seeds

For the dressing:
· 2 tablespoons Dijon mustard (grainy or fine grain)
· 4 tablespoons cider vinegar or white wine vinegar
· 5 tablespoons extra-virgin olive oil
· sea salt and black pepper, to serve

METHOD

· Combine the cabbage and carrot and caraway seeds in a medium salad bowl. Whisk the dressing ingredients together in a small bowl or mug. Drizzle the dressing over the cabbage and carrots, season to taste with sea salt and black pepper and mix well.

OVEN-BAKED CHIPS

SERVES 4

INGREDIENTS

- 4 large all-rounder potatoes (approx. 900g), such as Maris Piper, washed and peeled
- 3 tablespoons vegetable oil
- large pinch sea salt

METHOD

- Preheat your oven to 200°C/gas mark 6. Place 2 large greaseproof baking trays in the oven to heat.
- Cut the potatoes into long chips about 1.5cm thick and put them into a large mixing bowl. Drizzle with the oil and toss well, so all the chips are coated.
- Take your preheated baking trays out of oven and lay the chips evenly on them. Sprinkle with the sea salt and bake in the oven until they're golden brown, which should be about 30 minutes.

RED ONION GRAVY

SERVES 4

INGREDIENTS

- 2 tablespoons cooking oil
- 2 medium red onions, thinly sliced
- 1 tablespoon dried mixed herbs
- 2 tablespoons cornflour
- 850ml vegetable stock, cooled
- 1 tablespoon soy sauce
- 150ml glug red wine (optional)

METHOD

- Heat the oil in a medium, heavy-bottomed saucepan, then sauté the onions for about 5 minutes until they have softened. Stir in the mixed herbs.
- Meanwhile, put the cornflour into a jug and slowly stir in the cooled stock. Then slowly pour this stock into the saucepan with the onions, stirring constantly until all the stock has been well mixed in.
- Add the soy sauce and the red wine (if using).
- Simmer gently, stirring often, for about 10–12 minutes, until the gravy has thickened and coats the stirring spoon well.

BEETROOTS IN CRÈME FRAÎCHE

When I first started cooking with beetroots I used to peel and then boil them and then wonder why all the colour seeped into the water, leaving the beetroots looking drained. Then my mum showed me that if you leave on the skin to cook (boil or bake) them and then peel them afterwards, you retain the colour and the flavour.

I like the little squeeze of lime as it lifts the dish and gives an extra lightness to the flavours. This is the perfect side dish to accompany a hotpot or serve with a large chopped salad — or even at a barbecue.

SERVES 2

INGREDIENTS

· bunch fresh medium beetroot (approx. 500g)
· 3 tablespoons crème fraîche or soured cream
· squeeze of fresh lime or lemon juice
· 1 tablespoon chopped fresh parsley (optional)
· sea salt and black pepper, to taste

METHOD

· Preheat your oven to 180°C/gas mark 4.
· Wash the beetroot and stab the skin a couple of times with a knife or fork. Bake them, in their skins, for 1 hour until cooked through.
· Wait until they're cool enough to handle, but still warm (you don't want to burn your fingers), then peel and slice them thinly and place in a medium mixing bowl.
· Stir in the crème fraîche (or soured cream) and add a squeeze of lime or lemon juice. Mix well, and season with a little sea salt and some freshly ground black pepper. I like to serve this warm, but it can be eaten at room temperature.

SILKY CHOCOLATE SAUCE

This sauce has so many great uses! Drizzle it onto the Coconut Rice Pudding on p.206 or coat strawberries or brazil nuts with it. I also love this chocolate sauce simply spooned over vanilla ice cream.

SERVES 4

INGREDIENTS

· 100g plain chocolate (minimum 70% cocoa solids),
  or milk chocolate if you prefer
· 4 tablespoons single or double cream

METHOD

· Pour about 7–8cm water into a medium saucepan
  and bring to a gentle simmer.
· Break the chocolate into chunks and put them into a
  large heatproof bowl that will sit on top of the pan.
· Add the cream to your bowl of chocolate pieces.
  Then place this over the pan of simmering water,
  making sure the bowl does not touch the water, to
  gently heat the chocolate until it is just melted.
  Stir well and remove from the heat so It doesn't
  overcook. It should have a silky, glossy consistency.

TOFFEE SAUCE

This salty sweet sauce is completely delicious spooned over banana splits, as a topping to an ice-cream treat or served warm drizzled over baked apples, to name but a few options.

SERVES 4

INGREDIENTS

· 110g salted butter
· 110g light brown sugar
· 5 tablespoons maple syrup
· 200ml double cream

METHOD

· Gently heat the butter, sugar, maple syrup and
  cream in a small or medium saucepan until melted
  together and smooth.

DESSERTS
AND
BAKING

ORANGE AND LEMON CUPCAKES

I used to make these as vanilla cupcakes, but one day my eldest son requested something a bit different — so I came up with a citrus combination that has become a family favourite. I think the sweetness of the orange cupcakes complements the sharpness of the lemon-flavoured icing really well.

MAKES 12

INGREDIENTS

· 110g butter, softened to room temperature
· 110g caster sugar
· 2 large, free-range eggs
· 110g self-raising flour
· zest and juice of 1 large orange (approx. 3 tablespoons juice)

· 12 cupcake cases

For the icing:
· 30g butter, softened
· 250g icing sugar
· zest and juice of 1 large lemon

METHOD

· Preheat your oven to 180°C/gas mark 4. Line a non-stick muffin tin with 12 cupcake cases.
· Either with a wooden spoon in a large mixing bowl or with an electric whisk, cream the butter until it is fluffy, then beat in the sugar. Add the eggs, one at a time, whisking thoroughly. Gradually mix in the flour and beat well until the mixture is light in texture. Stir in the orange zest and juice. Beat together for a few minutes to make sure all is well combined.
· Spoon the cupcake mix equally between the 12 cupcake cases.
· Bake for 15–18 minutes, until the cakes are golden on top but still light and springy to the touch. Take them out of the oven and leave to cool.
· To make the lemon icing, put the softened butter into a medium to large mixing bowl, sift in half of the icing sugar and beat the two together. Mix in the lemon zest and juice, then sift in the remaining icing sugar and beat well. To finish, evenly spread the lemon icing onto each cupcake and they are ready to eat.

MY
BROWNIES

I couldn't really write a cookbook without including brownies. My schoolfriends used to love it when Mum made a fresh batch of brownies; these were very American and not that well known in the 70s and 80s in south-east England, although now of course they are famous worldwide. There are so, so many extras that you can add to brownies: chopped pecans or walnuts, broken-up pieces of white chocolate, dried cherries, and so on. But I have opted for a very simple recipe, partly because my kids pick out the nuts, and partly because I love them just like this — with cream or vanilla ice cream on the side for dessert.

MAKES APPROX. 16 BROWNIES

INGREDIENTS

- flour, for dusting the tin
- 100g plain dark chocolate (minimum 70% cocoa solids), broken up into chunks
- 150g butter, at room temperature, plus more for greasing the tin
- 200g sugar, preferably unrefined caster sugar
- 2 large, free-range eggs, beaten
- 1 teaspoon vanilla extract
- 70g self-raising flour

METHOD

- Preheat your oven to 180°C/gas mark 4. Butter and lightly flour a non-stick baking tin, about 23 x 23cm.
- To melt the chocolate, place the broken-up chocolate pieces in a medium to large heatproof mixing bowl. Sit it on a pan of gently simmering boiling water (the water only needs to be about 5cm deep). The moment the chocolate has melted take it off the heat and allow it to cool slightly.
- Meanwhile, in a separate mixing bowl beat the butter until it becomes lighter in colour, then add the sugar and beat well until it becomes light and fluffy. Gradually whisk in the beaten eggs and mix well. And now mix in the vanilla and the melted chocolate (making sure the chocolate is not too hot, as it may cook the eggs). Mix in the flour and combine well.
- Pour the brownie mixture into the prepared baking tin and bake for 12–15 minutes. Take it out of the oven and leave it to cool slightly, then turn it out onto a wire cooling rack or plate. The brownies should be moist and a bit gooey. Cut into squares or rectangles, and serve.

ARTY'S CHOCOLATE CHIP COOKIES

My eldest son loves chocolate chip cookies; this recipe is the first he made for me, hence the name. I think they are addictive — once I start munching them I find it so hard to stop, and the smell of home-baked cookies is hard to beat. If you want an extra citrus twist to these, you can add the zest of one orange when you're mixing in the chocolate pieces.

MAKES 18–20 COOKIES

INGREDIENTS

· 115g salted butter
· 60g golden caster sugar
· 1 large, free-range egg, beaten
· 1 teaspoon vanilla extract
· 170g plain or spelt flour
· ½ teaspoon bicarbonate of soda
· 175g plain dark chocolate (minimum 70% cocoa solids), broken up and bashed into little chunks (or milk chocolate if you prefer)

METHOD

· Preheat your oven to 190°C/gas mark 5. Line a baking tray with greaseproof paper or baking parchment — or use a non-stick tray.
· Cream together the butter and sugar in a large mixing bowl. Mix in the egg and the vanilla and beat well. Then mix in the rest of the ingredients.
· Spoon tablespoonfuls of the cookie dough onto your baking tray, spacing them out well, so they won't stick together as they expand in the oven, and gently flatten them slightly.
· Put them in the oven for about 10 minutes, or until they are lightly golden and just firm to the touch; they will harden up more once they have cooled.
· Leave the cookies to cool, preferably on a wire rack. Then eat!

CHOOSE-YOUR-OWN-FLAVOUR LOAF CAKE

It makes me happy to have a loaf cake on display at home, sitting on a glass cake stand. It's so welcoming. And the joy with this is that you can use the basic recipe and then choose the flavour you want depending on your mood: vanilla, lemon or chocolate — or whatever you like. For the one in this photo I made a vanilla cake mix and stirred in melted chocolate without mixing it in too much — to give it a marble effect.

SERVES 8

INGREDIENTS

- 200g butter, at room temperature, plus more for greasing the tin
- flour, for dusting the tin
- 200g sugar, preferably unrefined caster or granulated sugar (but regular caster sugar is fine)
- 3 large, free-range eggs
- 200g self-raising flour

Choice of flavours:
- I teaspoon vanilla extract
- OR zest and juice of I lemon
- OR 80g melted plain chocolate
- OR zest and juice of I orange

METHOD

- Preheat your oven to 180°C/gas mark 4. Butter and flour a 23cm non-stick loaf tin.
- In a large mixing bowl, beat together the butter and sugar, until the butter becomes paler and takes on the consistency of thick cream, then gradually whisk in the eggs.
- Now fold in the flour carefully. Add your flavouring of choice, mixing well, before pouring the cake mixture evenly into the loaf tin and smoothing over the top.
- Bake for 50 minutes, until the cake is golden on top and firm and springy to the touch.
- Take the cake out of the oven and let it cool in its tin for about 10 minutes. Then turn it out of the tin onto a wire rack or plate — and it's ready to eat!

LINDA'S LEMON DRIZZLE CAKE

This is a loaf cake that my mum liked to make and it remains a firm favourite of mine. The lemon syrup poured over the freshly baked cake seeps down into the sponge and adds a special moisture to the taste. Perfect to have with a cup of tea in the afternoon.

SERVES 6

INGREDIENTS

- 125g butter, softened, plus more for greasing the tin
- flour, for dusting the tin
- 150g caster sugar
- 2 large, free-range eggs, beaten
- finely grated zest and juice of 3 lemons
- 180g plain or spelt flour
- 2 teaspoons baking powder
- 4 tablespoons milk
- 50g icing sugar, sifted

METHOD

- Preheat your oven to 180°C/gas mark 4. Butter and flour a 23cm non-stick loaf tin.
- In a medium to large mixing bowl, cream the butter and caster sugar together with a wooden spoon (or use an electric mixer). Gradually beat in the eggs and mix until light and fluffy. Stir in the lemon zest, flour and baking powder, and mix well. Add 2 tablespoons of the lemon juice and mix well again. Then beat in the milk.
- Pour the cake mix evenly into the prepared loaf tin and bake for 45 minutes.
- In the meantime, mix the remaining lemon juice and the icing sugar together in a small bowl to make a syrup.
- When it's ready, take the cake out of the oven and leave it to cool in its tin for 5 minutes. Then turn it out onto a plate. Pierce the top of the cake all over with a thin skewer. Spoon the lemon syrup carefully and evenly over the cake until all of it is absorbed. Ready to eat.

PEACHES AND CREAM PAVLOVA

My second eldest son loves meringues, so we make this dessert together. It has a wonderful meringue base topped with sweetened vanilla whipped cream and ripe sliced fruit and works really well with seasonal ripe peaches or nectarines. But if you can't get hold of them, you can scatter a selection of fresh berries — such as blueberries, raspberries and strawberries — on top. Or, to make it more autumnal, sliced ripe pears with toasted pecans and grated chocolate on top works well too.

SERVES 6

INGREDIENTS

- 4 large, free-range egg whites
- ¼ teaspoon lemon juice
- pinch salt
- 1½ teaspoons vanilla extract
- 100g caster sugar

For the topping:
- 225ml double whipping cream
- 1 tablespoon icing sugar, sifted
- 1 tablespoon vanilla extract
- 3 peaches or nectarines, halved, stoned and thinly sliced

METHOD

- Preheat your oven to 140°C/gas mark 1. Line a large baking tray with greaseproof paper or baking parchment.
- With an electric whisk, beat the egg whites until they are light and airy and nearly stiff. Add the lemon juice, salt and the 1½ teaspoons of vanilla, and continue beating at a medium speed while adding the sugar a little at a time.
- Spoon this meringue mixture onto the baking tray and spread it out to form a round base about 15-18cm wide.
- Bake in the oven for 1½ hours, or until the outer part of the meringue is crisp. Set it aside to cool.
- In the meantime, prepare the cream and fruit topping. Whip the cream until it just stiffens and holds its shape, and then mix in the icing sugar and vanilla. You do not want to over-whip the cream.
- Smooth the whipped cream evenly over the top of the cooled meringue. Then decorate with the peaches or nectarines, in a design spiralling out from the centre. Ready to serve.

MAPLE SYRUP BAKED PEACHES AND APRICOTS

This is a yummy summer dessert for when peaches and apricots are in season. If you can't find both fruits ripe at the same time, you can just use either peaches or apricots. It makes for a sweet light pudding that I think works well after an indulgent meal.

SERVES 6

INGREDIENTS

- 6 ripe peaches
- 12 ripe apricots
- 2 tablespoons butter
- 6 tablespoons maple syrup
- 2 teaspoons chopped fresh thyme, leaves picked off woody stalks (optional)

METHOD

- Preheat your oven to 180°C/gas mark 4. Line a baking tray with foil or parchment paper.
- Slice the peaches in half and take out the stones. Then do the same with the apricots. Arrange the fruit, hollow side up, in the baking tray. Divide the butter into little pieces evenly between the hollowed-out peach and apricot halves.
- Drizzle the maple syrup over the fruit and sprinkle the fresh thyme on top.
- Bake in the oven for 25 minutes until bubbling hot and turning golden. This is heaven served with vanilla ice cream, or with cream poured over the top, or simply on their own!

PLUM AND PEAR CRUMBLE

Crumble is delicious and deceptively guilt-free, using a surprisingly small amount of butter and packing a whopping fruity punch. This crumble is also very versatile. You can play around with the fruit combinations, using apples and blackberries instead, or berries, depending on what is in season. This pudding can be served on its own, but is also great with custard or cream or ice cream.

SERVES 4

INGREDIENTS

For the filling:
· 8 ripe plums, cut in half and stones removed
· 4 ripe but firm pears, cored and cut lengthways into quarters
· 100g soft brown sugar
· 1 teaspoon ground cinnamon

For the crumble:
· 80g plain flour
· 50g porridge oats
· 50g ground almonds
· 50g soft brown sugar
· 100g butter, chilled and cut into cubes

METHOD

· Preheat your oven to 190°C/gas mark 5.
· Cut the sliced plums and pears into bite-sized pieces and put them into a medium baking dish (about 26cm). Sprinkle the 100g soft brown sugar and the cinnamon over the fruit and stir together well.
· To make the crumble, put the flour, oats, ground almonds and soft brown sugar into a medium mixing bowl. Then add the butter and gently rub these ingredients together, using your fingertips, until the mixture resembles course breadcrumbs.
· Scatter the crumble evenly over the prepared fruit in the baking dish.
· Bake for 45 minutes, until the topping is golden and crisp, and serve hot or at room temperature.

CREAMY CHOCOLATE MOUSSE

This rich mousse is great for a dinner party dessert, as it has quite a 'grown-up' dark chocolate edge to it. I like to add whipped cream to the recipe as it adds lightness to the mousse. And of course you could use a good-quality milk chocolate instead, to make it less 'grown up'!

SERVES 4

INGREDIENTS

- 150g plain dark chocolate (minimum 70% cocoa solids), broken up into chunks
- 30g lightly salted butter
- 2 large, free-range eggs
- 1 tablespoon sugar
- 150g double or whipping cream
- ½ teaspoon vanilla extract

METHOD

- Melt the chocolate and butter together in a medium stainless-steel or heat-resistant glass bowl set over a medium pan half-full of gently simmering water. Stir occasionally and once the mixture has melted, take the bowl off the heat and allow it to cool slightly so that it's warm rather than hot.
- Separate the eggs, setting aside the 2 yolks in a small bowl or cup, and then whisk together the egg whites and sugar with an electric mixer or hand whisk until they have set to a foamy consistency that can form soft peaks.
- In another bowl whip the cream until it too just forms soft peaks, and then stir in the vanilla extract.
- Once the melted chocolate has had a chance to cool slightly, stir in the egg yolks thoroughly. Now stir in 2 dessertspoonfuls of the whisked egg whites to allow the mix to become smoother, and then gently fold in the rest of the egg whites. You fold rather than beat them in, as you do not want to knock the bubbles and air out of the mix.
- Finally, lightly fold in the whipped cream and spoon equally into 4 ramekin dishes or small bowls or pretty teacups. Cover in clingfilm and keep in the fridge for at least 1 hour.
- I like to take the mousse out of the fridge half an hour to 1 hour before serving to give it a chance to come to room temperature again.

COCONUT RICE PUDDING WITH CHOCOLATE SAUCE

Rice pudding has always been a family favourite. We used to love it when Dad told us the story of how Mum learnt how to make baked rice pudding. When they were newlyweds, she kept asking what his favourite dishes were. He mentioned rice pudding. Mum had never made it before and she found a very complicated recipe that was a complete failure – she was so disappointed. So my dad called up our Auntie Jinny in Liverpool and she talked Mum through how easy and tasty it could be. We all loved it.

I cook this rice pudding in a saucepan on the hob, and the hint of coconut makes it feel delicately exotic. The desiccated coconut is an optional extra – I think it gives the pudding a nice texture, but if it's left out the rice has a creamy smoothness that is just as satisfying. The swirl of chocolate sauce on top transforms it into a good dinner party dessert.

SERVES 4

INGREDIENTS

- 100g Arborio, pudding or short-grain rice
- 400ml tin coconut milk
- 2 tablespoons water
- 4 tablespoons golden caster sugar
- 1 teaspoon vanilla extract
- 2 tablespoons desiccated coconut (optional)
- chocolate sauce, to serve (see p.175)

METHOD

- Place the rice in a large, heavy-bottomed saucepan. Pour in the coconut milk, then rinse out the tin with the 2 tablespoons of water and add those to the pan too.
- Bring to a gentle simmer, mixing well, and then add the sugar, vanilla extract and desiccated coconut. Now simmer gently, stirring often, for about 15 minutes, until the rice is just cooked through.
- Serve with a drizzle of chocolate sauce on top.

ICE-CREAM CELEBRATION CAKE

This is my favourite cake to make for birthdays. I buy the Madeira cakes, but if you want you can make your own (by following the loaf cake recipe on p.193 and using the vanilla flavour). It's a surprising cake, because it is iced, so it looks like a normal frosted cake until you cut into it and see the ice-cream centre. Kids and grown-ups alike devour it.

MAKES ENOUGH FOR 8 PEOPLE

INGREDIENTS

- 3 Madeira loaf cakes, shop-bought or home-made (see p.193)
- 5 x 100ml tubs ice cream of your choice (e.g: vanilla, chocolate, strawberry — choose your favourites or use 500ml of one flavour)

For the icing:
- 150g butter, softened to room temperature
- 450g icing sugar, sifted
- 50ml milk or warm water
- 1 teaspoon vanilla extract
- hundreds and thousands sprinkles, or other cake decorations of your choice

METHOD

- Line the base and sides of a 20–23cm, deep non-stick cake tin with baking parchment or greaseproof paper. Cut the loaf cakes widthwise into slices about 1.5cm thick. Then completely line the cake tin with the cake slices, slightly overlapping them so there are no gaps (make sure you leave aside some cake slices to lay over the top of the cake later). Using your hands, push the cake down into the sides of the tin.
- Allow the ice cream to soften so that it is easy to scoop out of the tubs. Spoon the ice cream, one flavour at a time, into the prepared cake-lined tin. Use your spoon to press the ice cream down. Repeat until the cake tin is filled with ice cream. Then layer the reserved loaf cake slices over the top of the ice cream and press them down firmly. Place a plate over the top of the cake, then put it in the freezer to allow the ice cream to fully freeze again — at least 1 hour, but you can leave it overnight.
- To make the icing, put the softened butter into a large mixing bowl, then gradually beat in the icing sugar and mix in the milk or warm water and the vanilla extract. Whisk together well until the icing is light and fluffy.
- When the ice cream has frozen hard again, take the cake out of the freezer and turn the cake tin over onto a plate. Peel away the parchment and spread the icing evenly over the cake, then put the cake back in the freezer until you are ready to serve it.

NUTTY SWEET PIE

This is a tasty variation on a traditional pecan pie — which I love — but this makes a nice change and is delicious served with cream on the side or a scoop of vanilla ice cream melting on top. For the pastry, you can use my Shortcrust Pie Pastry recipe on p.166, and the golden, nutty filling is quick to throw together.

SERVES 8–10

INGREDIENTS

· 300g shortcrust pastry dough, home-made
  (see p. 166) or shop-bought
· flour, for dusting work surface
· 125g butter
· 2 tablespoons golden syrup
· 100g soft brown sugar
· 1 teaspoon vanilla extract
· 300g coarsely chopped mixed nuts (such as brazils,
  walnuts, pecans, almonds, hazelnuts)
· 2 large, free-range eggs, lightly beaten

METHOD

· Preheat the oven to 180°C/gas mark 4. Get out a metal pie dish (or use a 23cm fluted metal flan tin with a removable base).
· Roll out the pastry on a clean, floured surface to a thickness of about 3mm, in the shape of your tin, drape it over the rolling pin and then lay it carefully into the tin. Trim off the excess pastry and then chill the pie base in the fridge for half an hour. Line the base of the pastry shell with greaseproof paper and pour in some baking beans or rice (for blind baking the pastry). Bake the pastry shell for about 10 minutes in the middle to lower part of the oven. Then remove the baking beans or rice and greaseproof paper, and bake the pastry for a further 10 minutes, or until it is a light golden colour. Take it out of the oven and set aside to cool.
· In a medium saucepan melt the butter and golden syrup together. Turn off the heat then mix in the soft brown sugar and the vanilla extract. Add the nuts and mix well so they are well coated in the sugary melted butter. Allow the mixture to cool slightly, then stir in the beaten eggs. Mix well, then pour the filling into the waiting pastry case.
· Bake for about 35 minutes, until the pastry is golden brown and the filling has set, but is still a little soft. Let the pie cool a little before serving.

DELICATE APPLE TART

My step-grandmother first showed me this recipe when I was in my early teens, and I still love to make it today. I think of this tart as quite graceful, it doesn't need to try too hard. The ingredients are few, but the taste is wonderful.

SERVES 6

INGREDIENTS

For the pastry:
- 300g plain or spelt flour
- 160g unsalted butter, chilled and cut into cubes
- a little butter, at room temperature, for the tin
- ¼ teaspoon sea salt
- 4–5 tablespoons cold water

For the filling:
- 4 or 5 apples (use crisp eating apples, not cooking apples)
- 50g salted butter
- 3 tablespoons caster sugar, preferably unrefined
- 100g apricot jam (I use St. Dalfour jam)
- I tablespoon water

METHOD

- To make the pastry, put the flour, chilled and cubed butter and the salt into a medium or large mixing bowl and mix with a spoon or knife until all of the butter is coated with flour.
- Add the water and now mix with your fingertips, kneading just until the mixture all comes together to form a ball. Take care not to overwork it; pieces of butter should be visible in the pastry (and will give it a wonderful flakiness). Wrap the pastry in clingfilm and refrigerate for at least I hour.
- Preheat your oven to 170°C/gas mark 3. Butter a large, thin baking tray, measuring about 30 x 40cm.
- On a clean, lightly floured surface, roll out the pastry to a thickness of about 3mm, to the shape of your baking tray. Lay the pastry around the rolling pin and unroll it onto the tray. Keep it cool in the fridge while you prepare the apples.
- Peel and quarter the apples, remove the cores and then slice the apples thinly. Arrange the thin apple slices on the pastry in a neat, overlapping design (like the pattern of tiles on a roof), leaving a 5cm border around the edges, then fold the pastry edges in over the apples to form a frame.
- Dot the butter evenly over the top and then sprinkle with the sugar.
- Bake for 60–75 minutes, until the pastry is well cooked and crisp and the apples are browned.
- In a small saucepan melt the apricot jam on a low heat with I tablespoon of water mixed in, then brush this over the apples. Ready to serve.

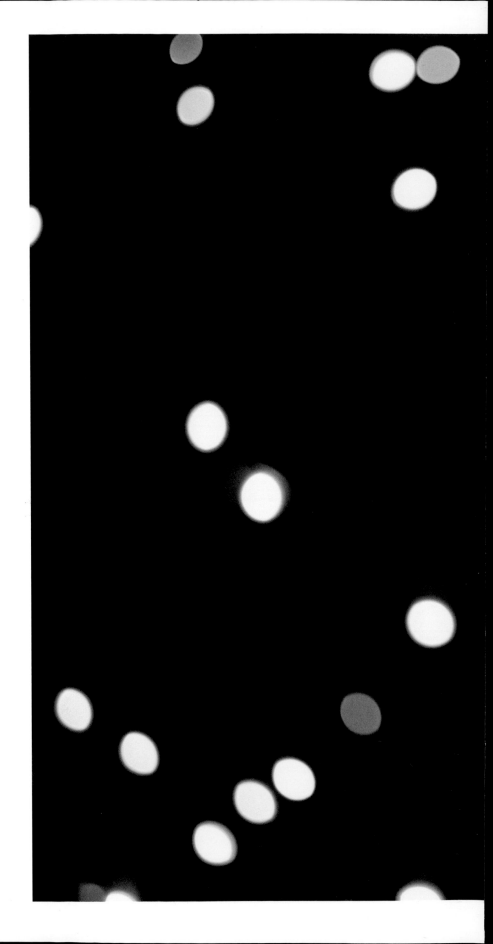

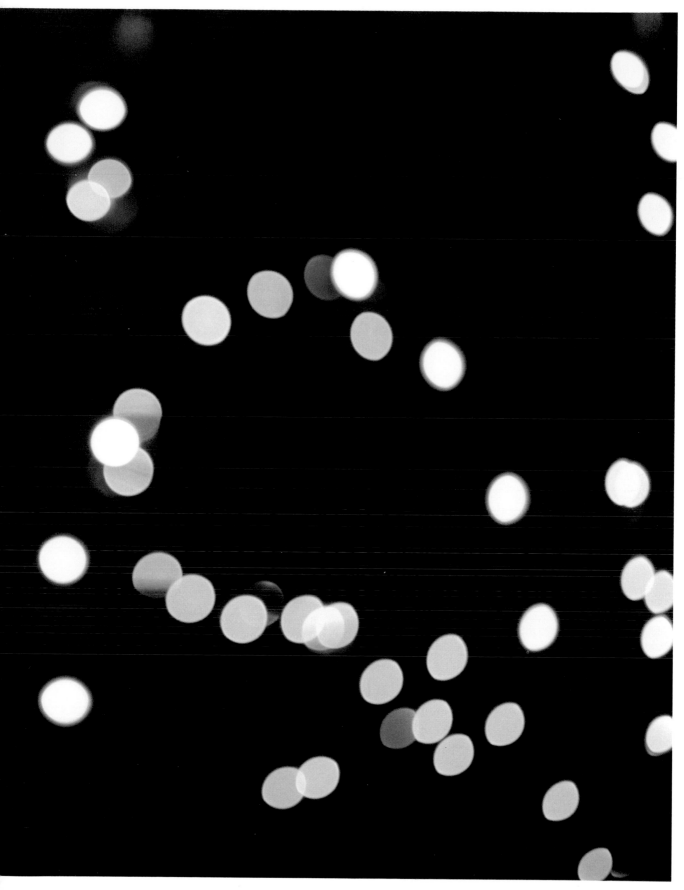

ACKNOWLEDGEMENTS

I would like to say a big thank you to Sam, Caroline and Sha for their invaluable help and patience. For Mum for the memories that made this book possible and Simon for nagging me to do it. Thanks to Dad, Arthur, Elliot, Sam, Sid, Hettie, Stella and James. To my cousin, Lee, for his advice. To Olivia for the use of her wonder garden, to Gillian at Judith Michaels and Daughter for lending me crockery for photos, to Mark for putting me in touch with a great publishing team. To Sean for the lovely prints. To Aunt Louise and Maxine for ideas, and to Kasia, Brown and Michelle.

INDEX

For my family, for eating, talking, laughing and inspiring